EMOTIONAL PROBLEMS OF ADOLESCENTS

Emotional

Problems

of ADOLESCENTS

J. Roswell Gallagher, M.D.

and Herbert I. Harris, M.D.

THIRD EDITION

New York   OXFORD UNIVERSITY PRESS   1976

To C. D. G. and E. W. H.

with deep gratitude
for their constant understanding and encouragement.

Foreword to the Third Edition

Mol an óige agus tiocfa sí.
('Praise youth and it will prosper.')

This book is for parents, teachers, and club leaders, and for those counselors, ministers, nurses, physicians, nurse practitioners, and medical students who advise and care for adolescents. Its third edition includes entirely new chapters; the others have been extensively revised.

Basic information is provided about boys and girls themselves: their development, their personality traits, their problems, the stresses they face, their needs, and ways to help them with, and to prevent, their difficulties. The intent is to offer a basis for an understanding of them and their personal and emotional problems in plain, nontechnical language.

Sexual permissiveness, the drug culture, and behavior therapy are but a few of the remarkable changes and innovations that have occurred since this book was first published sixteen years ago. One would think that changes of this magnitude would produce comparable changes in adolescents but, as testified to by Kiell's anthology of great writings about adolescents from the time of Socrates to the present, one is struck by the similarities in the behavior of adolescents from century to century.

Desirable as it is that adolescents be encouraged to take increasing responsibility for their lives, and to work out their own problems, there are times when they need and may seek help. When these situations arise, an informed person can be of great assistance; furthermore, an informed adult earlier will have *prevented* many of the problems.

Basic to helping an adolescent of either sex is the process of communication. Often an adolescent's whole life style can change when he is able to confide in an adult, and the burden of feeling is shared. Ways to talk to these adolescents, and ways to help them, at least temporarily, are discussed. Throughout this book *listening*, because of its value and their need for it, is emphasized.

The adolescent boy or girl is a *person*, not a *problem*. It is this individual who needs to be understood, not the failure in school, the stealing, the anxiety, or the drug abuse. We trust, too, that our readers will remember that many of the problems which plague both adolescents and the adults who deal with them are universal and are weathered by most adolescents without much assistance and with little damage.

Adolescents' emotional and behavioral problems baffle their parents more than they do other adults because the close ties between parents and their children make it very difficult for them to be objective. At the same time, however, since many adults temporarily may, in an adolescent's mind, slip into his parents' place, these others may also have to deal with all the bewildering vagaries of behavior which confuse and upset parents. So it is that teachers, ministers, or coaches become involved in the adolescent's rebellion, infatuations, cheating, drinking, or suicide attempts. They, and other adults who can and do play such important roles in young people's lives and development, will be most helpful—and least likely to become uneasy and frustrated—when their insight into adolescents' behavior is based upon a knowledge of what young people are like.

That sort of knowledge we have tried to set down in this book in the hope that it will help parents and others to prevent adolescents' problems from becoming incapacitating, reduce adults' bewilderment, and increase the effectiveness of adults' efforts to help young people to become mature citizens. We cannot give directions as to how this or that parent or other adult should 'change' in an effort to solve some boy's or girl's problem. The personality and emotional ties are unique in each instance and are too varied, too involved, to justify any such directives. Usually it is the adolescent's feelings which must change— it is he who must learn to adapt himself to things as they are. Often the most important gesture a parent can make is to remain steadfast and consistent so that as the adolescent strives to become an adult he feels that at home he has a solid and predictable, even if not ideal, base. In short, it is not a question of parents and other adults learning to modify their *behavior* which is of primary importance: it is that they increase their *understanding* of young people.

As this book's title implies, it is about problems. While it has been the experience of most student health services that no more than 10 per cent are even briefly handicapped by the conflicts which arise as they progress from being children to being adults, we are sure that a wider understanding of young people's needs and characteristics and of ways to prevent their more serious difficulties will come from a discussion of their problems. This is not to say that knowledge of these problems in themselves is an unworthy goal, but rather that we feel it is a limited one, and one not as rewarding as an effort to increase our understanding of each adolescent.

Adolescents *are* different. They are no longer little children, and they are only beginning to be adults. *They* differ from each of those; and *we* need to think differently about them when we try to understand them and their problems.

Wisdom

*is the principal thing; therefore get wisdom:
and with all thy getting, get understanding.*

Proverbs IV:7

CONTENTS

EMOTIONAL PROBLEMS OF ADOLESCENTS

1

THE NATURE OF ADOLESCENCE

The nature of adolescence has changed little since ancient times. Compounded, as it is, of the sensitive wonder of childhood, the energy of youth, and the succession of physical, mental, and emotional changes that occur in these years, adolescence—the period in life when one is in the *process of becoming* an adult—is the most astonishing period of life. Bernard Shaw regarded youth as so wonderful a time that it seemed a shame to waste it on young people!

Nevertheless, many adults find the fact of adolescence more perplexing than wonderful and some, perhaps recalling the problems of their own adolescence, tend to adopt a protective attitude toward young people and to forget that 'the sweet uses of adversity' are no less important to the developing adolescent than they are to the adult. If adolescents are to develop into stable, mature citizens able to meet the demands of adult life, they must learn to cope with difficult experiences by themselves. The adult's role is to set a good example, to be understanding, to listen, and to lend adolescents a helping hand *when it is needed*, not to be too quick to think for them, to do for them, or to protect them.

It is not only those young people who reach adolescence laden with troubles that began in early childhood who now may need understanding help: others, apparently well adjusted previously, may now find it difficult to clear one or another of the hurdles which optimal development requires that they surmount. They must try to shed their narcissism and acquire concern for others, gain independence in thought and action, and yet gradually come to understand interdependence, come to terms with their sexuality, achieve their identity, and eschew arrogance as they increase their patience and their capacity for empathy. Adolescents are not yet mature—they are only striving to be: maturity is slow to come to many.

Clearly, the better we understand these changes and strivings and stresses, and the better we understand the problems which beset all young people, the more effectively can we help them ourselves and help them to obtain the proper kind of assistance. Some adults intuitively say and do just the right thing to tip the balance in a troubled adolescent's favor, while others, though better informed, may fail to help at all. How you *feel* toward them can be a more determinant factor than what you *know* about them, for there is a world of difference between understanding *adolescence* and being genuinely interested in an *adolescent*. Nevertheless an adult who is interested in young people and feels sympathetic toward them will be able to do more for them as he acquires a wider knowledge of their traits, needs and problems.

Those among the adolescent generation whose personalities and future effectiveness are threatened have still the hope of change for the better. Soon their malleability, their capacity for change, will be largely lost: adolescence is the last of the age periods in which we can expect success from other than the most expert and prolonged efforts to strengthen the personality and character and to build emotional and physical health. This importance of seizing the opportunities adolescence offers cannot be stressed too strongly. It is the time to try to remove those incapacitating fears which still persist, to modify those feelings and attitudes that hinder emotional growth, to encourage the strengthening of conscience. These are still the adaptive, imitative, pliable years: before long, habits will become so fixed and feelings so deeply repressed that it will be much more difficult to straighten them out.

It is because we know that many teachers, doctors, ministers, counselors, and camp and club workers have a deep interest in adolescents that we have written this book for them as well as for parents. We hope that it will aid them in the salient part which they all play in young people's development.

As a basis for understanding adolescents one must know something of their physical characteristics. Despite the fact that they differ widely from one another, they all follow the same pattern of physical development and have for the most part similar needs and problems growing out of this general pattern. One matter which is of great interest and concern to them and which frequently effects their happiness and behavior, is the growth and development of their bodies. Any minor blemish or defect is regarded by the adolescent with much more interest and worry than it warrants. A minor degree of acne, protruding ears, small breasts, a facial scar, or a supernumerary nipple may seem insignificant to parents or a physician but can be the cause of a surprising amount of anxiety for a boy or girl. Many of course will take these in their stride, but some at this stage of emotional development find nothing about their bodies trifling or amusing: their appearance, which they formerly ignored, now keeps them glued to any mirror they chance to come upon.

Small children and adults have little emotional concern about their size. An eight-year-old child does not care much how tall or grown up he is, and a thirty-two-year-old adult does not become emotionally upset by the fact that his height is greater or lesser than his neighbor's. The adolescent, however, feels differently. Height, weight, and degree of sexual maturity all mean a great deal to him. The adolescent who is not maturing as rapidly as his or her companions, the boy who is shorter, or the girl who is taller or more obese than the others, dislikes being this different and may become emotionally upset by fears of getting even taller or fatter or never maturing. Some of this preoccupation with size and maturity is due to adolescents' need to conform, to be like their peers. Some of it arises from the fact that both factors are important in athletics, in social success, and in assuring acceptance by their own age group. Some of it develops because for years parents, teachers, and physicians have expressed such great interest in their development, checking their measurements against charts and standards which children accept unquestioningly even though often they fail to understand, even actually misinterpret, them. At times their preoccupation and anxiety arise because they imagine that their harmless masturbation, in which they nevertheless persist, may be affecting them adversely.

Few adolescents are aware that wide variations from the average are compatible with normality: to most of them, to vary from what is average is to be abnormal. They need to understand that many different states and rates of growth and development are normal.

As their bodies develop and change, so do adolescents' interests and attitudes develop and change from those of their earlier years. When the adolescent was an infant the crib measured the limits of his world. Next, his playpen, later his backyard and his own home held all he had to understand. Then, a boy, he entered that wonderful carefree time of climbing fences, teasing girls, collecting everything, rising early, yelling, playing ball—a time of shyness, stuffed pockets, and despising soap.

Now he is beginning to be an adolescent. Girls—suddenly taller and more mature than he—are no longer ignored, well-cut clothes are more desirable than a bulging pocket, and clumsy feet show intermittent promise of coordination, he sleeps late, and only when offguard or with his group does he shout or let himself go. He is before a mirror almost as often as his sister. They themselves—their appearance—assume more and more importance to them. Their narcissicism is in the ascendancy. The approach to sports is more professional.

Those are the little changes. The major ones in adolescent girls and boys are their wanting to be grown up, their need for success, their striving for prestige and acceptance by their group. Later will come concern with their sexuality, rebellion against authority, increasing ability to conceptualize with its accompanying idealism and questioning, neglect of and rebellion against family, loyalty to their own friends, questioning of what they once accepted on faith, and concern with their own identity and shedding of their narcissicism. Yet for all this striving, their efforts vacillate. An adolescent will let his first glamorous date wait while he shows a friend a new rifle. He may be fearful, at the end of a hard-fought struggle for independence, of accepting the freedom he has won. His sister, a grown-up party date one night, the next day tries to outswim her brother.

Much of this ebb and flow of the changes of adolescence comes from confusion in trying to settle on which parent to model their behavior. It would seem a simple matter of boys following father and girls their mother; but the fact is that this matter of being attached to and wanting to please and imitate a parent can be one of the more disturbing processes of adolescence. The implications are clear. A girl is more likely to want to grow up to be feminine and to take on the responsibilities of a wife and mother if her own mother is one she admires and whose happy life makes marriage seem to be a state to be desired. The boy whose father goes at life with zest and pleasure is encouraged in the desire to grow up to assume adult responsibilities. When parents lack such attributes it should not be surprising to find girls and boys preferring not to grow up and trying in a variety of ways to be as unlike a parent as they can be.

If there is one thing to remember about adolescents it is that they are greatly concerned about their own personalities. They want passionately to be themselves, to achieve their own identity. They are so preoccupied with developing their own personalities, so on guard against being taken advantage of, and yet so vacillating in the capacity to be themselves, that one cannot hope to deal with them successfully unless one recognizes this preoccupation and pays as much attention to *them* as one does to whatever it is that one is trying to advise, teach or to correct. The adolescent is so aware of the importance of developing himself—his own personality—that he instinctively resists any effort of yours to impose your will or your ways upon him, though, left alone, he may imitate you. In short, an adolescent is more aware of his own personality than is a child, and less willing to sacrifice part of himself than is an adult. The wise teacher recognizes this and teaches each *student*—not just history or mathematics. Similarly, the experienced physician treats his *patient*, not just the diabetes or the heart murmur. It is well to remember that adolescents are particularly responsive to anyone who is genuinely interested in *them* and their ideas. After all, they have had years of being told what to do, what is right, and have had little chance to state their own ideas without meeting quick criticism. The gains that can come from listening to them, from asking their opinion, and from avoiding impatience, preaching, sarcasm, and authoritarianism should be obvious. For some adolescents the search for answers to 'Who am I?' and 'Where am I going?' may be a long and painful one.

Matters associated with sex, and achieving independence together with that search for identity are the chief tasks of every adolescent. On the way toward their goals, boys—and an increasing number of girls—in this age group go at things strenuously. They want success and recognition desperately, and *moderation* is not in their vocabulary. For this reason, prescriptions involving rest and restriction should be avoided unless they are really warranted, and then should be accompanied by patient, thorough but brief explanations, *and* by an effort to provide compensatory interests. It is usually better to emphasize strengthening these young people for renewed activities than it is to suggest that rest will relieve their fatigue. Furthermore, in evaluating their fitness (of their hearts or knees or backs, for instance) it is well to bear in mind the strenuous way they live.

Their sexuality is one of their most baffling concerns. They are physically mature, their sexual urges are at the highest point in their life span, and they are confused by what is preached and what is practised. The sexual freedom arrived at by the access to new contraceptive methods is far outside what would have been considered the limits of acceptable behavior fifteen years ago. Now, the number of unmarried couples cohabiting is legion. Countless "campus romances" continue throughout the undergraduate years and often lead to marriage. Among the members of the counterculture, the unmarried girl living with a man is a standard fixture, except for homosexuals. Among the latter, thanks to the new ruling of the American Psychiatric Association and the work of the Mattachine Society and the Gay Liberation Front, the emotional tensions which rejection brought to them have been greatly diminished.

Young people's sexual relationships today often serve as a means of forming a more satisfactory emotional relation. The anomie that has developed in our society afflicts our adolescents almost more than it does adults. Whatever has caused the inability to communicate among our younger generations, it has been observed that, in a reversal of the usual patterns of intimacy, sexual intimacy has frequently led to the growth of much more general and effective communication among them. It may well be that the disparity between the bodily maturity of adolescents and their slower emotional development has been responsible for the rejection by society of sexual intimacy among them.

No less important to adolescents are their changing relationships to their parents. It is the time of breaking away from home, of trying to stand independently, of temporarily leaning on friends as they rely less on their parents and still hesitate to stand alone. Vacillating both in their desire and their capacity to be independent, but apparently unaware of how dependent we all are on one another and how essential cooperation is, neither they nor their parents behave in a consistent or very dependable manner. Often those who scorn their parents most, and are most rejecting of them, are the insecure ones who find the parting from their parents the most difficult. It is as though only by denying how important their parents are to them can they bear to tear away. It can be a trying time for them, and equally so for an anxious, insecure, possessive parent who fears for them and therefore clings to them.

Rebellion is so common and what lies behind it so important that we must say a word in praise of this at times disturbing phenomenon: the crude and exasperating behavior of those young people who find this stage in the transition from utter dependence to independence so difficult. We should all bear in mind that conformity and dependency, though less apt to disturb the peace, may in reality promise only unhappiness and ineffectiveness for the years of adulthood which lie ahead.

The adolescent's imperative need to achieve independence cannot be overemphasized. As young people grow up, they should have increasing opportunities to try their own wings: these they now need as they formerly needed adults' constant protection and support. To continue to protect them now, continually to thwart their attempts to develop independence, is to rob them of the abilities, confidence, and resiliency they must have in the challenging and unpredictable adult world. They will make mistakes; they may not do as well alone as they could have done with help, but they must learn to do for themselves. Most of them instinctively realize this fact and rebel when these opportunities for 'solo flights' are denied them.

This, and such questions as death, religion, fallen heroes, and conflict between their parents are crucial factors when one is trying to understand an adolescent. By bearing them in mind, by remembering that these are the kinds of problems which confuse and upset them and lie behind much of their baffling behavior, we stand the best chance of helping them.

If it is realized that these people are becoming more mature and are beginning to think about vital issues and to question older people's behavior, it will be obvious that an adult's conduct in relationship to them should be very different from what it used to be. They are no longer just little people, to be scolded, to be *told*, to be protected. Now they are old enough to be encouraged to have opinions, to take responsibility, to make decisions. Having produced children, we must show confidence in them if we are to help them become mature men and women.

The more we can do this, the better will our adolescents cooperate—and the greater will be our contribution to their well-being. This does not mean that parents no longer play a role. They do, and a very important one—but it differs greatly from the role they played with the little child who primarily needed their protection and love. Now the adolescent needs to do for himself, and to feel that you are backing him but not in charge of him, advising him only when really necessary, and confident in his improving judgment and his ability now to profit from his inevitable mistakes. So, while adults must realize that their suggestions and warnings may be interpreted by the adolescent as evidence of little confidence in him, thereby increasing his own anxiety and diminishing his small store of confidence in himself, they must bear in mind that striving for maturity is not the same as having achieved it. Until adolescents are really confident and independent they like to feel that help and moral support will be forthcoming when needed. This new role for parents and other adults who deal with adolescents is not always easy but it won't be too mysterious or too difficult for them if they accept the fact that as young people change, so must adults' roles change.

To build confidence, to strengthen their egos, adolescents need to be trusted, and they need the happy experiences and the recognition which achievement and success bring. There are few adolescents who do not get their full measure of criticism and failure: almost all would benefit from more trust and praise and more success. The Irish have a saying full of wisdom: *Praise youth and it will prosper.* Given such encouragement, in time they will 'find themselves,' will abandon their enveloping concern with themselves and develop that degree of concern for others that, along with the ability to defer gratification of one's wishes and hopes, abandon arrogance, and accept our dependence on one another are the hallmarks of maturity. None comes easily or quickly.

We have been setting forth some of the usual problems and characteristics of adolescents, the kinds of changes and questions which most of these young people face and conquer. These are matters for many of us—not just for their parents—to remember; for during these years of beginning to be an adult and giving up being a child, which is what adolescence really is, young people are breaking away from home. So when parental impulses prompt one to try to help the adolescent to mature, one may experience only rebuff, hurt feelings, and bewilderment. Yet this is also a time when they may turn for help to other adults with whom there are no close emotional ties and so little embarrassment. With this advantage, the teacher, doctor, minister, counselor, coach, and club leader are in strategic positions to give valuable help.

We know but few of the answers. While no one knows them all, we shall try in this book to help others see through the vagaries, problems, and inconsistencies of adolescents to their essential selves. We shall discuss in detail some of the emotional disturbances that beset adolescents, but we emphasize that acquaintance with these conditions is important chiefly because of the clues they convey for preventing less severe but related upsets.

There are few rules and few generalizations to aid adults in helping adolescents, and, valuable as it is, a wide knowledge of the psychodynamics of human behavior is not essential. But some facts, a thorough acquaintance with methods of going about helping young people, and a clear picture of one's objective will make your genuine desire to help the adolescent (which is of prime importance) more effective and more rewarding.

2

THE IMPACT OF ADULTS
UPON ADOLESCENTS

In infancy and early childhood the influence of parents is paramount, but as children grow older their peers, relatives, neighbors, and other adults have ever-increasing influence upon them. The qualities of these adults, their personalities, their steadfastness, their understanding, their leadership are powerful factors in the adolescent's emotional development. The physical needs of young people are usually given attention, but what adults can say and do to foster their emotional development is too often overlooked.

Mental and emotional health is our cardinal problem. It disrupts more lives than physical illness. Parents and teachers who have great emotional impact on adolescents and who direct young people for many hours of their day, can play an impressive part in the prevention of mental illness and in the early detection of emotional disorders. Furthermore, they can be invaluable in the management of those everyday problems which may be warnings of later trouble. Others to whom this book is directed are in touch with young people for fewer hours, but they, too, play an important role.

In the 'surging sixties' when revolt and protest enlivened almost every college campus, the word on students' tongues was 'relevance.' *Relevance* was the cry of emotion-starved adolescents for more *feeling* in the many dry-as-dust courses that were taught by men and women who had long before left much of the *'life'* of their subject behind them to go on to more esoteric and recondite areas in their field. The result was to be expected. Students were bored, failed to 'catch fire' over topics reviewed year after successive year and found their adolescent rebellion against 'the teaching establishment' stirred all the more powerfully.

When a subject is dull it is for one reason only: the instructor is failing to put his heart into its communication. 'Heart' or feeling is the drive, the vital force, in the transmission of knowledge, whether it be by parent, coach, clergyman, club leader, or physician. So, although so much of this chapter is devoted to the influence of the academic teacher on the adolescent, the comments apply equally to other 'teachers.'

Educators are agreed that the teacher's primary function in this area is preventive: to keep young people mentally healthy. Increasingly they emphasize the importance of teachers being as familiar with the principles of mental hygiene as they are with the subjects they are employed to teach. This philosophy is founded on the belief that it is the school's function not only to teach the curriculum, but also, by action and by example, to help as many young people as possible to flourish and to master the art of good human relationships.

Few nowadays dispute the primary importance of developing well-balanced personalities, or deny that to teach a *boy* or *girl* is more important than to teach a *subject*. Some people, however, are skeptical of the part which nonprofessionals should play in the prevention of mental and emotional illness. However, the physicians, psychiatrists, and psychologists cannot alone solve our mental health problems. All adults should learn more about its causes so that they will be alert to those problems which assail so many essentially normal young people and which, ignored or permitted to worsen, may lead to distress or disaster. Many of these difficulties can be helped at home or in school in a friendly way, without psychologists or psychiatrists. Specialists should be on hand to advise and guide teachers and others, but their exclusive care should be reserved for those more seriously upset.

Familiarity with the principles of mental hygiene not only makes the teacher or parent, clergyman, club leader, physician, or coach a potent ally in the fight against mental illness but also improves the effectiveness of teaching itself. Some teachers who would seem to have discouraged a young person may have stimulated him to outstanding success. A skating instructor, for example, is said to have told Dick Button that he would never be a great figure skater. Dick refused to believe him and went on to win more awards for figure skating than anyone else ever had.

Learning, however, in adolescence is enhanced by encouragement and the creation of a friendly, relaxed atmosphere. The boy or girl who feels secure, who has good relationships with both his parents and his teachers, learns best. A student's "I do my best in history; my teacher is terrific" is a meaningful comment. The teacher who practices the elementary procedures of mental hygiene can be expected to command respect and to make his pupils wish to please him.

A schoolroom, club, or home which is relaxed and friendly does not mean one in which boys and girls can do as they please. Leadership is essential to adolescents, and they should learn early to distinguish between liberty and license. They don't want to be pushed around, but they need and like a firm, respected adult in charge. "My math teacher? She's o.k.; she's strict but she knows her stuff, she's fair, and she really seems to want to help us to understand math." In their girls' or boys' clubs they look to the director, in the troop to their scoutmaster, on the playing fields to their coaches, in their school to their principal and teachers for this leadership, but the leader must be capable, honest, just, and genuine. Young people are quick to detect feigned interest: they can detect a phony a mile away.

Years ago, when large families were the rule, the father was the leader. Like the captain of the ship he plotted the course, sailed the ship, and stood off threats to the safety of his crew. The principal of a school stands in a comparable position: to a lesser degree attitudes of dependency upon him develop in both his faculty and his students. Just as they resent and rebel against high-handedness in their father at home, and feel insecure and anxious when he is weak and vacillating, so do boys and girls resent and rebel against any invasion of their rights and prerogatives and show evidence of poor morale when they lose confidence in their teachers' or their club leaders' ability and judgment. The emotional ties, the rivalries, the struggles for affection and recognition resemble those which are found in a family. They differ only in degree, being most intense in the boarding school, less obvious in a large day school from which everyone goes his way at nightfall, and minimal in the club which is visited only periodically.

The emotional tone of a school is determined in part by the caliber of its principal, but its overall climate is much more the sum of each classroom-teacher's attitude toward his or her students. This climate clearly reveals the teacher's own emotional tensions and maturity. For example, a teacher who suffered much loss of parental attention when younger siblings were born may appear harsh and very much the martinet with his or her pupils because of long-buried envy and rivalry toward younger children. These are deep and powerful feelings, even though they may have been repressed so long that they may seem to have been forgotten. Surges of repressed emotions may arise in one who faces a class which revives memories of early childhood jealousies and defeats.

An unhappy, sarcastic, upset teacher recalled an incident from her early life which illustrates this point. On returning home from her grandmother's, where she had stayed for three weeks when her baby brother was born, she rushed to his crib, not with the curiosity one might expect, but in a truly savage wish to kill the infant. This old, undispelled rage festered in her unconscious far into her adult life, warping her attitudes toward men, toward her pupils, and even toward her own child. It is not common to elicit such dramatic evidence, yet we can be confident that similar though less extreme buried feelings can influence the classroom behavior of some teachers and the daily actions of many adults.

Young people's responses to such a teacher are as predictable as they are undesirable. Though she was competent, honest, and faithful, Sally's teacher could not seem to resist every opportunity to criticize her, to be sarcastic, to hold her up to ridicule. Sally's early innocent efforts to please her brought no praise. It is easy to understand why Sally soon was saying, 'I won't study. I won't go to school. I hate her!' Teachers who, driven by unconscious need, are fearful or retaliatory will arouse a student's wholesome anger.

The interplay of personalities in the classroom is no less dynamic than in the home. In school there is a constant interaction between student and teacher, variously interpreted by different teachers. To some the class seems to be a threatening monster, to others a volcano ready to erupt.

Such was the case of a young instructor whose unconscious was filled with long-repressed hostility toward a younger brother. His classroom manner was halting, tense, and painfully insecure. He would correct tests with a sharp pencil with which he would jab any mistakes he chanced to discover; later he admitted that it gave him a feeling of "ha!—I've got you!" In class his palms would sweat, his throat and mouth would become dry. At night he even occasionally dreamed of being chased by hordes of students. His anxiety stemmed from his fear that his students would discover his unconscious hatred of them, and retaliate. Fortunately, after he had begun to understand his feelings, his relationship to his students, his attitude toward his work, and his effectiveness as a teacher all improved strikingly.

The club leader or teacher who feels that his groups are like active volcanoes may prove to have been pretty much of a 'sissy' as a child, one who lived in mortal terror of the 'roughnecks' in the neighborhood. Now an adult, he or she finds that the boisterousness of the aggressive youngsters revives the old terror of the rough kids who terrorized him or her when small.

Endless varieties of early experiences, defeats, and disappointments play a part in determining an adult's emotional reactions to adolescents and so vitally affect his relationship with them. Envy of brothers or sisters, an unhappy adolescence, a thwarted desire for another career, all these may provoke harsh behavior which the adult regrets and fails to understand. On the other hand, a man predominantly influenced during his adolescence by his mother may show a feminine solicitude which provokes anxiety, for tenderness is not in the masculine tradition and can cause confusion and uneasiness in boys. On one occasion a student came to his doctor in a state bordering on panic: he was not eating, he was losing sleep, was unable to concentrate on his studies, and gave every appearance of a boy suffering from intense anxiety. As he talked more and more about his trouble, the name of one of his club leaders occurred with increasing frequency. Slowly he approached an awareness of the fact that this adult's attentions and considerate treatment of him at first made him grateful but that later feelings had been awakened for him which had some of the qualities of an adolescent's first love. Slowly the boy began to see that what had happened was that much of the love and devotion he had had for his mother had been transferred. The homosexual implications in such a state were the roots of his anxiety. When he came to realize these emotional goings-on, it became relatively easy for him to distinguish between his mother and the motherlike club leader and to regard the latter with relaxed objectivity.

Club leaders and teachers, no less than coaches, parents, doctors, or clerymen are neither ogres nor saints; they are only very human, with the faults and virtues of us all. They are like all of us—rigid *and* flexible; tolerant *and* impatient; happy *and* maladjusted. Their behavior stems from their pasts and is determined by their own inner security. It is because of their close relationship to and their strong influence on young people that it is particularly essential that we and they see beneath the surface aspects of their behavior to its motivating springs.

The understanding adult regards adolescents as a group of individual personalities, growing and developing as they alternately agree and disagree with him and with each other. He is not afraid to build rich relationships with them and encourages disagreement and debate; he makes no claim to omniscience; he regards the approach of each as a new personality whose acquaintance he is about to make.

Teachers' attitudes and behavior are of more influence in forming a student's taste or distaste for education than are the subjects they teach. There is truth in the cynical warning that teachers must at all cost avoid destroying a love of learning.

However, it is no more important to remember that all adults exhibit human frailties than to remember the remarkable resiliency of the adolescent. For centuries boys and girls have withstood the thrusts of many unhappy adult personalities, and yet each generation has produced its crop of scholars, scientists, and lovers of the arts. But even so, in these days of multiple pressures and in the face of the astronomical statistics for mental illness, our world's desperate need for learning, and our world's need for emotionally well-balanced adults, it is essential that thought and attention be given to every force, whether conducive or inimical, that bears upon emotional health.

The teacher, though very important, is only one of the forces affecting young people's mental health; but few adults are privileged to know the satisfaction of that large group of teachers truly respected by successive generations of students. Though an adolescent's praise is usually laconic and colloquial, it is no less heart-warming to hear that a boy or girl has said that his teacher is 'terrific.'

3

ADOLESCENTS' SEXUALITY

Since this book was first written, tremendous changes have taken place in society's attitudes toward sexuality. Havelock Ellis and Bertrand Russell were voices crying in the Victorian wilderness of prudery in advocating a more open approach to sex and a kindlier understanding. Old attitudes die hard and it should be remembered that in spite of the efforts of Siecus, the Mattachine Society, and numerous societies for birth control and abortion there persist in many areas numbers of people for whom sex is still a 'dirty' word and its discussion taboo.

Despite the new freedom, practically every adolescent faced with the imperious demands of the sexual drive develops some degree of anxiety. A boy may find himself uneasy and bewildered over nocturnal emissions, 'wet dreams' ('nocturnal pollutions,' the sex advertisements call them, adding to the guilt which surrounds sex). A girl may experience her first menstrual period—menarche—without having been adequately informed about this natural process, and become anxious and upset as a result. Members of both sexes may experience guilt and anxiety over masturbation: an activity which actually focuses their sexual energies where they belong and precludes their deflection into perverse and emotionally unhealthy channels.

Even as recently as a few years ago ideas about masturbation were appalling from the standpoint of their capacity to produce neurotic sexual behavior. On this subject, J. E. Horrocks wrote as recently as 1962: 'Among the ills attributed to masturbation have been overfatigue, loss of weight, loss of potency, cancer, ulcers, loss of athletic ability, loss of social competence, insomnia, death, insanity, feeble-mindedness, pimples, bad breath, weak eyes or loss of sight, paleness, stooped shoulders, neurasthenia, dizziness and susceptibility to disease.'

These old wives' tales about sexual experience linger. It is not surprising, for adolescents, lacking information and embarrassed to ask, are as likely to accept the false as the true. Even today we find college students who are guilt-ridden and deficient in overall effectiveness because of their struggle to stop masturbating. These puritanical attitudes persist in our culture to the extent that adolescents still developing a good working conscience regard the pleasurable feelings associated with anything sexual as sinful and therefore 'bad for you.' Consequently, masturbation, common to animals and openly practised by children in simpler cultures than ours, can severely disturb misinformed and guilty adolescents. But after they have had a chance to ask questions, and be reassured, the sense of relief they feel and the consequent change in their entire behavior can be dramatic.

It is to be regretted that so few parents are able to talk freely about sexual matters with their children. This lack of freedom probably derives from the old erotic ties that develop between the parent and child in infancy and which are revived for a time in their adolescence. Where this is the case, parents should arrange to have some well-qualified person provide their children with pertinent facts and wholesome attitudes toward sex.

A study of the origins of masturbation is revealing. Greatly stimulated by the rise in sexual hormone levels in the blood that occurs at puberty, masturbation represents another of the many regressive forces of behavior common to these years. In boys, the regression is to the old, intense attachment to the mother which so strongly influenced his behavior in the years of his infancy. Those who would understand adolescent boys should be aware of the struggle between their need to emulate their fathers in order to develop a predominantly masculine ego, and their reluctance to give up the femininity of their mothers which they acquired as small children in copying (i.e. loving) mother. They are torn between the desire to be masculine and the wordless fears that threaten their efforts to take upon themselves a man's behavior, actions, and responsibilities.

In girls' development masturbatory activity is less common than it is in boys. When similarity to the mother has been accepted and the drive to be like her grows, the girl appears to direct her attention and feeling toward her whole body rather than to the specific genital area. This difference may account for the greater emphasis woman has placed upon fashion in dress and hair styles and other ornamentation of the body. However, emphasis upon such items may lessen with the continuing development of women's liberation, but we must bear in mind that in the eighteenth century men's fashions were flamboyant, far outshining the relative restraint of women's styles. So far as we are able to determine,—and no careful studies of this matter are to be found in the scientific literature—the incidence of masturbation in girls who have difficulty in accepting a female role similar to their mother's (the tomboys) is not greater than in those who accept the feminine role.

Much more perceptive scrutiny must be given to the male and female roles and their distinctive characteristics. There is suggestive material, elucidated by Erikson, workers at Yale, Piaget, and others, that at either end of the masculine-feminine spectrum, clear sexual differences can be observed. However, male dominion over the female has obtained for so many centuries in our culture that it may be many more years before truly feminine temperamental and intellectual differences can be adequately delineated. The forces that led to the equal rights amendment in the United States and the advances in recognition and status achieved by the women's movement promise that much more free expression of the feminine spirit will appear in the future.

What influence these changes will have on the adolescent female can only be speculated upon at this writing. The unisex trend that developed several years ago may be said to seem to have diminished of late, and, of course, the inexorable facts of child-bearing still exert their influence on the lives of young people. Wider understanding of the emotional concomitants of pregnancy should give us much more adequate basis upon which to delineate the differences of the sexes.

Masturbation will, of course, continue, though in some cultures it may be less general because of earlier engagement in heterosexual activities which those societies permit.

While no physical ill-effects result from masturbation, emotional ills may develop when the practice arouses guilt or fear: although feeling guilty, the boy or girl who continues this activity may then become increasingly anxious and worried. When there is a fear that some personal harm is being done, a kind of autosuggestion may take place: masturbation is then accompanied by the thought, 'I am hurting myself.' Instead of the adolescents deriving erotic pleasure from the act, unconscious impulses to punish or harm themselves are being reinforced.

Such impulses are not uncommon in adolescents and may be neurotically directed toward rendering themselves less manly, or less womanly.

Masturbation representing an apparent desire to make oneself like a member of the opposite sex is uncommon, but it is found to a degree in some young people. The deep infantile urges to be like the mother a son loves are not easily resolved. This is usually true when not to become a man would mean relief from the threat of resembling a father whom he dislikes. So, too, may arise the daughter's deep desire to be like her father and to escape being like her mother, and so to escape womanhood with its burdens and responsibilities. The thrust of adolescent energy at this time is to break the old infantile urges of boys to be like their mothers and girls to be like their fathers. The less a boy leans toward his own sex, the more he will tend to feel like a woman and may behave as one toward his own sex; and the less a girl leans toward her own sex the more she will act like a boy and avoid things feminine. When their development stops here, some youths may drift into homosexuality.

To enter into activities which can yield them prestige and peer acceptance will help many young people during this time when they are adjusting to heightened intensity of feeling and learning to live comfortably with new drives and relationships. This is not to imply that they can solve these problems by immersing themselves in a ceaseless round of activity, social, academic, or athletic. But to occupy their minds with satisfying and acceptable pursuits is clearly healthier than a preoccupation with a guilt-ridden obsession about their sexuality.

For the anxious adolescent, male or female, the essential fact of the harmlessness of masturbation must be underlined. It becomes a source of worry in those who believe it to be harmful yet are unable to desist, so that their guilt becomes even greater. When emotional tension surrounding masturbation is a reflection of an adolescent's difficulty in growing up to be like the parent of his or her own sex, opportunities to get authoritative information, to have questions answered, and to talk out worries should help. The opportunities to build a friendly and admiring relationship with an adult one would like to emulate, and to experience achievements which bring praise from contemporaries of the same sex may also be of value.

The chronological age at which boys become physically mature varies greatly. Some at fourteen are capable of reproduction; others show little evidence of secondary sex characteristics at sixteen. Consequently it is reasonable to expect considerable variation within a group of adolescents of the same age in their heterosexual interests and impulses. The aggression, the power of the sexual drive, and the preoccupation with sex evident in a boy who has matured early may lead him to sexual intercourse, whereas such behavior is beyond the thoughts, the desires, and the capacity of his less mature contemporaries. For the most part, the younger adolescents' heterosexual experiences are fragmentary and sporadic, and are less frequent in those whose interests and economic status enable them to remain in school than those of the same age who quit and take jobs. Adolescents who are less fortunate economically or intellectually may use heterosexual activity as a way of acting as an adult, and in order to compensate for their scholastic shortcomings.

Mature sexual expression is the goal for adolescents, and during these trying, compromising, impulsive years the adolescent needs the good example and guidance of understanding adults. It is just as important that all things sexual not be tinged with guilt and indecency in their minds as that they avoid entanglements which would overtax their emotional stability and capacity for responsibility. They are most likely to reach a satisfactory solution if they can see this problem for exactly what it is: a compromise which gives the fullest possible attention to the emotional health and happiness of others as well as to their own, and at the same time approximates the demands of the society in which they live.

Several influences deter adolescents from heterosexual activity. For the male, the tie to his mother and his unconscious fear of his father are important factors. The continuing attachment to the mother causes many boys to treat all girls as if they were symbols of the mother and consequently taboo. An even more powerful deterrent is their self-love or narcissism: they tend to regard themselves as perfect and not to be despoiled. So much has sexuality in our culture been associated with the body's excreta that many adolescents tend to regard any activity associated with the genitals as unclean.

Then, too, despite the sexual liberation of recent years, persisting mores of our culture restrain adolescents from heterosexual activity. Since much of the point of view of our religions is derived from the experience of the race, it is likely that this restraint has its roots in sacred hygiene: the ancients recognized that children born of adolescents rarely showed the vitality and intelligence of the offspring of fully mature parents.

Running counter to the forces of restraint and moderation are the many ways in which the sexual theme is exploited. Most obvious of these is the use of the erotic in advertising. The seductive female figure has long been exploited in the selling of every kind of commodity, with the implication that desirable females will fall into the reader's arms if he buys the product. The stimulation given to an adolescent's erotic daydreams is not likely to cool his already strong impulse to experiment with sex.

Movies, too, bombard the adolescent with sexual subject matter. Formerly, the Greek dramatic device of having climactic action occur off-stage was employed, serving to invest the sexual act with the heightened unreality of the daydream. Our present-day standards make it possible for older adolescents, at least, to observe most explicit adult sexual activity. What influence this will have on the sexual activity of adolescents in future generations remains to be seen. It is possible that the sexual freedom provided by 'the pill,' the I.U.D. and various other contraceptive modalities, may eventually bring about a much healthier climate in the sexual unfolding of adolescence.

Since rebellion against authority is so much a part of adolescence, and efforts to break the ties of dependence on parents perennial, the admonitions and the forbidding attitudes of parents about sex often stimulate a desire to flout them. Even as the small child, during the period of testing his own powers, says 'no!' to everything said to him, so do adolescents tend to deny the worth of adult attitudes. By the time they have reached adolescence they have learned many ways of saying 'no' to parents and to others of the older generation. Some young people, apparently compliant and docile, break out into the most unbridled kind of behavior whenever the opportunity offers. Nothing really vicious need be present in such an activity; it is more a graceless throwing off of the parental yoke. Adolescents, having only a sketchy knowledge of sex, may use clandestine experimentation as a means of expressing rebellion.

Adolescents feel the need to copy grown-up behavior in every way possible. By doing things adults do they feel more grown-up themselves. They consider smoking, drinking, and heterosexual activity, as well as staying up late, leaving school and taking a job evidence of being grown-up. A sexual experience is regarded as especially adult, because of the unique emotional conflict they are trying to work through. Struggling with the masculine and feminine elements in their makeups, or fighting for social acceptance by more mature and popular boys and girls, a sexual experience becomes not so much a goal as a means to an end.

A boy may think a sexual experience will serve both to

prove his masculinity to his doubting self and to win acceptance
from those who have not admitted him to their circle. The need
for acceptance on the part of a boy or girl is so intense that it is
very difficult to change a deliberate set toward sexual experience: only if rapport and respect have developed will the adult's
opinion be accepted. But once having won the esteem of an adolescent, it becomes easier to emphasize the importance of a
true love relationship which demands deep and sincere involvement and sharing, and convincingly to describe these as being
totally unrelated to the transitory spasms of the sexual act of a
tense and frightened adolescent. When adult love is adequately
described and interpreted it may then become easier for the adolescent to recapture the idealism he has lost: the idealizing of
love has given rise to much of the beauty in the cultural tradition of the Western world.

The problems of sex should be treated frankly and openly
whenever they arise. Sex education should begin when the
child is very young. It should be given in small amounts for
they can then absorb only simple, brief answers. Later sex instruction should not be deferred for one long momentous 'talk.'
Adolescents need, however, much more than some facts about
anatomy and physiology. They need even more to know the
social implications of sex, the contribution it makes to family
life. Their attitudes toward sex are more important than a
knowledge of anatomical facts. When mystery is removed from
sex and an effort made to free it from its associations with bodily
excreta, and when they recognize its role within their own and
others' families—its part in happy family life—we can more res-
sonably expect the idealistic adolescent to behave in an emotionally healthy way.

Most parents still find the discussion of sex with their offspring difficult, for they are, for the most part, emotional prod-
ucts of the traditions of the Victorian era. Their attitudes toward

sex die hard. Today we have a conflict with that thinking: contrary attitudes have developed out of the new psychology, out of the transcultural contacts which occurred during both world wars, and out of the extension of horizons which modern transportation and the communication media have brought about. For these reasons and partly because 'sexologists' and psychiatrists have moved in different orbits and have had difficulty integrating and disseminating new knowledge, a sound overall view of sexuality does not prevail even among the most youthful of today's parents.

It is most important that all adults who deal with adolescents have a mature attitude toward sex themselves. The sexually well-adjusted person is in control of this powerful force; the immature one, although perhaps seeming to be effective, is preoccupied by sex, not master of it. Mature sexuality embodies, in addition to the powerful physical urges that are necessary for man's survival, many factors which are derived from our earliest emotional experiences. These include, for example, the fact that the emotional ties of our infancy and early childhood for our parents are gradually diluted by the increasing number of attachments to other people—siblings, other relatives who may live in the house, and then playmates and neighbors. Later, when a lover is found, an emotionally mature person has more than the early experience with mother or father love to call upon. Experience with the less selfish emotional links to friends and associates enables mature love and marriage to approximate the ideal experience expressed in the language of the arts.

In contrast to the circumstances of mature love, the emotionally immature person, while maturing physically, has been unable to rid himself of the impulses of infancy and childhood. The sexually promiscuous male, for instance, is often one who has never given up his childish attachment to his mother. Such an attachment gives rise to strong desires to be feminine like her, urges the fulfillment of which is frowned upon by his male companions who are made anxious by any hint of femininity in a male. Driven by these forces, and unaware of their nature, he strives desperately to prove his masculinity by what he hopes will be considered a virile form of behavior—promiscuity.

Promiscuity is not common in adolescents, but it does occur. During adolescence, boys and girls work at shedding the need to be like the parent of the opposite sex, a legacy from the years of infancy. This is a continuing process which is not an accomplished fact at a given age: it makes adolescence a particularly crucial time because, if the change is not largely accomplished during these years, the attachment to the parent of the opposite sex may become so fixed that the adolescent will find it difficult in later life to play the part of father or mother, husband or wife, in a wholesome, emotionally mature manner. This unresolved conflict over their sexual role is accompanied by other immature patterns of behavior which will usually make both a marriage and its offspring unhappy and full of tension.

Fortunately most adolescents welcome the recognition of their need to be more masculine or feminine, and value highly any effort designed to encourage its satisfaction. Schools which have an active and popular social program and which encourage the younger as well as the older students to participate often greatly help their adjustment. Also helpful are small discussion groups, led by an understanding adult, which provide young people with a chance to express conflicts troubling them, and to discover that their problems are not unique.

Several factors clearly inhibit premature heterosexual experience. There is, for example, the commendable restraint which a healthy attachment to one's parents, and what they symbolize, provides. Then there is the unfortunate deterrent arising from the association of things sexual with things unclean, the result of poor or scant sex education. Operating against these restraints are influences like advertisements and movies, which keep sex in the forefront of adolescents' minds, and the adolescent's need to prove to himself that he has grown up. But the reaching of a saturation point may reduce sexual commercialism; and the latter urge can be met by treating the adolescent as if he *were* grown up, and by encouraging him to engage in other activities which might give him prestige: nothing helps more than an association with parents and other adults whose good example the adolescent will wish to imitate and whose esteem he or she cherishes.

Despite the increasing heterosexual activity among adolescents in the U.S., it is well to bear in mind that a high percentage of adolescents lead continent heterosexual lives. They dream, they idealize, and they masturbate. They pass through periods of emotional upheaval and pain over their sexual urges, but most of them emerge from adolescence with much the same attitudes and strengths of character as the preceding generation.

A small segment fail to work out of their childhood sexuality (the so-called polymorphous perverse sexuality of the latency period—the years from 6 to 12) and become latently or actively homosexual.

The undue excitement some people exhibit when homosexual behavior is discovered in some boy or girl often reveals more about their own anxiety about homosexuality than it does a concern over the young person's problem. The fact of the matter is that all of us are mixtures in various proportions of masculinity and femininity: few great people fail to have some strong element of the opposite sex in their temperaments. It may be that the inner conflicts which develop out of these people's special mixture of masculinity and femininity add fuel to their creative fires and contribute to the production of even greater works of art, science, or philosophy. At any rate it is not surprising, though it may be disconcerting, to find that in the course of their development, some adolescents sometimes drift into *transitory homosexual episodes.* The important matters are that these *transient* episodes be understood for what they are, and require different management from the treatment of true homosexuality.

The present-day widespread acceptance of homosexuality may very probably reduce the tensions surrounding it. This does not mean that it should be encouraged in the adolescent male or female. The idea that a high degree of unresolved femininity in a boy or masculinity in a girl may have desirable aspects ignores the mores of our society which derive from the need to perpetuate the race. The homosexual man or woman, and those with a high degree of identity with their own sex, do not, as a rule, have children. That there is now a comfortable place in society for these nonreproducing people is well, though much of mankind's history goes counter to the idea that theirs is a state to be encouraged. Yet in their own way homosexuals contribute to population control, and the reported rise in homosexuality may represent one of Nature's means of aiding this effort.

Parents, teachers, club leaders, and others of their own sex attenuate excessive femininity in a boy or masculinity in a girl by their power to inspire imitation of themselves. Hero worship is a healthy concomitant of adolescence. Boys and girls often wish to emulate an older person of their own sex, and they may find it easier during this age period to admire and copy someone outside their family. This kind of association, and the satisfactions from interests in activities appropriate to their own sex, help to resolve a hesitant orientation to the adolescent's own sex. Deprived of such influences, they may find themselves rejected by their peers and consequently drift more and more

away from the usual attributes of their own masculine or feminine condition.

These adolescent conflicts may give rise to behavior that
may alarm the unsophisticated parent. A boy who behaves ef-
feminately at this age, or the girl who imitates her male peers,
should not be confused with the true homosexual. Since all of
us vary in the degree to which we are masculine or feminine,
we should bear in mind that such admixtures are not indices of
homosexuality. The rather 'pretty,' not very athletic, unaggres-
sive boy should no more—on the basis of such traits—be labeled a homosexual than the football player. The unfortunate
aspect of such effeminacy is that such a boy, lacking the
strength and skill that would give him companions and recognition, may be shunned, labeled a homosexual, and be forced to
fill his needs for companionship by associating with those who
have no other friends—or perhaps with true homosexuals.

No matter how well they understand it, parents find even a
solitary episode of homosexual behavior very disconcerting.
There is always the fear that this is not a transient thing. A person with more professional training and experience than the
parents, and one less emotionally attached to the boy or girl, is
better fitted to judge and handle such a problem. Usually a
frank discussion of the situation and an opportunity to correct
any sex misinformation and to explain the childish and even infantile nature of this activity make a good beginning: an adolescent usually responds well to this kind of approach. Few adolescents wish to remain childish in their behavior, so the thought
that persisting in such activity might hinder maturity as an adult
often results in a powerful rejection of homosexual behavior.
Whoever counsels an adolescent in this fashion will do well to
continue the relationship with the boy or girl in order to discuss
interests appropriate to their sex and the general matter of heterosexual relationships.

Frank homosexuality is uncommon in boys or girls. Psychological theory postulates an arrest of emotional development in the true homosexual at about the fourth year of life. At this time, most children are still emotionally attached to the parent of the opposite sex,—boys to mother and girls to father. In normal emotional development, the fifth year of childhood inaugurates the onset of the emotional struggle to give up attachment to the parent of the opposite sex and to cleave to the parent of the same sex as a model for one's subsequent behavior. In cultural patterns in the U.S. this is far from being completely successful. Indeed, it has been remarked that much of the emotional conflict experienced in adolescence derives from the failure of many adolescents to have worked out those feelings during the appropriate fifth to seventh years. These young people try to meet the new and turbulent changes of adolescence still beset by conflicts that should have been settled long ago. As a consequence, many adolescents are gripped by emotional turmoil that is regressive and untimely,—it should have been resolved when he or she was six.

The adolescent boy or girl who comes from a home with parents emotionally immature, self-centered, and incapable of expressing true paternal or maternal love and care for their children may have great indecision about which parent to copy. Having been deprived of the warm love which is as important in infancy as food, they tend to convert their own capacity for loving into disturbing behavior in adolescence. For such people are emerging from the emotional poverty of their infancy and childhood and, without wholesome inner controls, are beginning to respond to the intense physical urges of adolescent sexuality. Having been able to love only themselves during the most critical years of their development, they are now able to love only those like themselves—those of their own sex. This is another of the origins of true homosexuality. Such a person, despite an outward veneer of adult behavior, is unable to develop and maintain the wholesome ties of love and affection so essential to mature emotional health.

There are not, fortunately, many parents of this type and, furthermore, numerous children born of such parents are spared a homosexual adaptation by favorable and compensatory factors in their environment. Consequently there is not a high incidence of true homosexuality in our society, but variations and gradations of homosexuality occur frequently enough to make the problem one of significance.

Factors which encourage homosexual behavior and those which discourage it need to be borne in mind. For example, a monosexual boarding school or college, all male or all female,—can encourage latent homosexuality. Here at an impressionable and malleable period of life, teachers, coaches, and others are in a position of strong leverage to influence the emotional growth of boys and girls. Similarly, although the matrix for trouble will have been laid down before they reach the secondary school level, the adolescent with homosexual tendencies may be attracted to the latently homosexual teacher. Teachers of this kind, some harsh, some kindly and mother-like, appeal to boys and girls who have personalities like their own. Having been conditioned to imitate the feminine side of their families, boys find themselves accepted by such male teachers and a justification for their feminine impulses. It is remarkable that only on rare occasions have such associations led to seduction by one or the other individual.

It is not known whether the influence of the Gay Liberation Front in developing a wider tolerance and acceptance of homosexuality will increase the incidence and prevalence of true adolescent homosexuality. For the most part, effeminate male teachers and masculine female teachers provide qualities of the opposite sex (which they act out) less threatening than the harshly masculine or tender feminine personalities of the more sharply defined faculty members. For in this period of adolescence when they are not yet emotionally prepared to accept all the demands of their gender, the relatively nonthreatening attitudes of teachers of this stamp give adolescents valuable emotional support. When the latent homosexuality of the teacher remains controlled, he or she may be among the most valuable members of the teaching staff. Intolerant attitudes toward the latently homosexual teacher reveal an utter lack of self-awareness and understanding on the part of members of the school's faculty and administration and is unfortunate for both the student body and the institution as a whole.

One situation must be treated with the utmost care when it arises in connection with a teacher, camp counselor, or club worker. We refer to accusations of perverse activity made by a boy or girl. On the one hand, it should be remembered that long experience shows that the majority of practicing homosexuals have found that it is of crucial importance to restrict their practices to fields far from home. Discovery and scandal can so easily occur in school or club or camp that sophisticated homosexuals are most careful to avoid gratifying their urges with those young people who come in contact with them in the course of their daily work. And on the other hand, if these situations are to be judged properly, it must be remembered that in adolescence the imagination is at its liveliest and daydreaming at its peak. An adolescent's imagination may well convert unconscious fantasies of his own into a belief that he has had a real association with some adult to whom he is attracted. Like children who believe their own imaginings, the adolescent may convince himself of the reality of something which exists only in his own dream life. For this reason, their evidence, though sometimes founded in fact, must always be weighed with great caution and with this possibility kept in mind.

These then are some of the emotional problems which sexuality poses for the adolescent. Most girls and boys reach solutions, some need a little help, and a few require expert assistance. All of them are materially aided in this period of adjustment when they have a strong and healthy relationship with the parent of the same sex from birth and subsequent appropriate relationships with other adults. Given support of this kind most adolescents will achieve a mature sexuality with few scars and little anxiety.

4

ACHIEVING INDEPENDENCE: REBELLION AND DEPENDENCE

'I just can't manage Bill; he pays no attention to me; he's positively defiant. Sometimes he just doesn't answer and sulks; at other times he slams the door and goes out. But no matter what, he plain ignores me and does as he pleases. You'd think at fifteen he'd at least have better manners. I don't know what's gotten into him; he didn't used to be this way.'

Rebellion becomes a problem when the natural development of a young person's independence meets with consistent opposition. Adults want young people to grow up and to become independent, but do not always seem willing to let them try. They forget that by continuing to help them they rob them of opportunities to learn to do for themselves. And when young people rebel, their defiance baffles and infuriates. Yet rebellion, though admittedly more difficult to live with, is really more praiseworthy and less frightening than is behavior which reflects a desire to remain dependent. All who work with and want to help young people need to understand rebellion: both adolescents and their parents may need help. It is often not an easy time for either.

The adolescent's imperative need to achieve independence, the gradual evolution of his behavior from the utter dependence of infancy toward the independence of adulthood, and the reasons for rebellion require as much understanding as do those essentials, love and security, which have for so many years been the basis of countless articles on the rearing of little children. That repetition is deserved: today too many people are handicapped by anxieties fostered by unhappy, insecure early years. However, the fact that young people should have increasing opportunities to become independent needs just as much emphasis. These opportunities they now need as they formerly needed constant protection and support. It is natural and proper for them to rebel; their rebellion is a problem only when it has to fight its way against parental domination and oversolicitude. To continue to protect adolescents, continually to thwart their attempts to develop independence, is to rob them of the abilities, confidence, and resiliency they must have in the demanding and unpredictable adult world they face. Later, secure and really independent, they will—we hope—be strong enough to realize how dependent we all are upon one another, how closely intertwined are our own safety and happiness with everyone else's. Continually to help adolescents is constantly to remind them that we have no confidence in their ability to learn to take care of themselves.

Bill caused his parents very little trouble or anxiety in his first fifteen years. Then during his second year of high school, things began to change, and a few months later his frantic mother sought help from his guidance counselor. 'I can't figure Bill out; he ignores me; he acts as if he thinks I'm stupid, sometimes as if he hated me. I can't understand what's gotten into him. We do everything for him—we get him anything he wants. We try to help him with his schoolwork; we're careful what friends he makes; we don't let him wear himself out doing jobs after school. He used to tell me everything. Now, if I ask him where he's going, all he says is "Out," and if I try to find out whom he's been with, all he answers is "Some of my friends." I tried for months to get him to have his teeth attended to before I finally gave up. Just last week we got a bill from the dentist: Bill had gone to him by himself and had never said a word to us. He's going around with some girl; I guess she's all right, but he won't bring her home. He won't talk about going to college. . . . Funny thing, though, every once in a while my husband and I get the feeling that he wants to talk—he sort of starts to and then seems to change his mind.'

That's adolescent rebellion, but to name it doesn't contribute much to understanding it. Obviously not all rudeness or defiance stems from a blocking of efforts to become independent: any person frightened and driven to distraction from any cause is apt to revert to frantic behavior; but when there is evidence that an adolescent's attempt to grow up is being consistently thwarted, rebellion is a normal and desirable, though unpleasant, phenomenon. Bill's behavior, if he were your Bill, would be hard to regard as desirable, but an adolescent's continued acceptance of overprotection can eventually cause even more unhappiness.

Living with another being in the process of achieving its independence is not always a happy experience. Bill started out totally dependent, literally tied to his mother. When he first tried to walk, it was with his hand in hers; slowly he broke away until he could walk by himself. This first evidence of his being able to do for himself made his parents very happy. They would have been very upset if he had not walked as early as Aunt Gertrude's boy, and they welcomed and applauded his early steps even though they were very awkward and even though he frequently fell. As he grew he gradually strove for more and more independence. Much later, now an adolescent with the size and strength to do a man's work, he wanted to be treated like one; he wanted to do his own schoolwork, choose his own friends, earn his own spending money, develop his own interests, have his own ideas. But his parents feared to have him try. They doubted his ability, his responsibility, and his judgment; and they believed it better for him to rely on theirs than to trust and develop his own. They feared he would make mistakes, would stumble; they feared he would make the same mistakes they had once made; and they dreaded the thought of his growing up and the thought of the time when he would need them no more. They forgot that his own awkward efforts would do him more good in the long run than the perfect things he could do with their help. They forgot that a transition from dependence to independence is normal, natural and something very much to be fostered. So they thwarted him—and he rebelled.

Rebellion is neither to be tossed off as "just adolescence,' to be laughed at, to be infuriated by, or to be cried over. Certainly it is not to be met with stiff resistance. It needs to be understood as unpleasant evidence that a natural desire to grow up, to become a self-sustaining individual in one's own right, is being sought, albeit in a very awkward fashion. It is important to understand what is behind it, what it is heading toward, and why you feel about it as you do. Parents have an essential role in the development of these young people. We understand *that*, and we realize that children need our love and protection, that they be made to feel that they are wanted and that they be made to feel secure against inevitable threats. But as these young people change and grow up, *adults' roles, too, must change.* They must relax their protection and give young people ever-increasing opportunities to do for themselves. Their real job is to produce an adult, not a child. Children begin this life utterly dependent and utterly selfish: as they grow they must leave these unenviable states and attempt to reach the opposite poles.

Parents must occasionally assess the part their emotions play in their attitudes toward their children and attempt to discover what is behind their wishes and their plans for them. Is it their own shortcomings and failures that must be erased by their children's achievements? Are these successes ones the young people desire or have the aptitudes for, or are they only their parents' unfulfilled dreams? Is it parents' fears which force them always to think only of the dangers which threaten their growing son or daughter? Are their restrictions and restraints deeply colored by their own anxiety and insecurity? Is it their own emotional need for their children that makes parents fear to let them grow up, leave, and strike out alone? Is this the basis for their secretly wishing that their child not grow up? Is it their children's faults, or just the shadows of the parents' own faults which they think they see in them, which make parents worry for the future? At this time when parents are being alternately renounced and sought by them—when their chilldren at one time awkwardly strive for independence and next fear to accept it—it is hardly strange that parents alternately wish them to grow up and try to push them into maturity and then, fearing they are not ready to accept responsibility, refuse to let them try. By understanding this—how the parent feels and why, and what the boy or girl needs—an adviser can do much to help hold the family together and to foster the boy's or girl's maturity.

Not only parents but also teacher, coach and youth leader need to watch that they do not retard the young person's maturity. 'He would do better in college if he postponed college a year.' Perhaps it would be *easier*, but might it not be *better* for him to test his strength? Or he may want to give up football. Well, after all, isn't his new interest in chemistry more maturing than football? So when his interest wanes and he begins to deprecate his activity, give him freedom—or give him responsibility.

The female is traditionally the less aggressive sex, but girls also need to develop their individuality and to gain independence. Thwarted in her efforts to grow up, a spirited girl becomes rebellious and can upset a home as completely as can her brother. When Mary was fourteen, a year after her father died, she and her mother were at swords' points. She refused to help with the housework when her mother asked her to, but occasionally when her mother would go out she would return to find that Mary had cleaned the house from top to bottom. The neighbors couldn't believe that Mary refused her mother's requests, that she was disobedient and impertinent, and that she never talked to her mother about her friends and her activities. She chattered endlessly to some of these neighbors and frequently helped them with their household chores. The telephone and Mary's going off on dates without permission caused the most violent scenes. Sometimes, when a boy would telephone Mary, her mother would would fly into a rage and snatch the receiver from her.

Mary became more and more surly and evasive and stayed away from home more and more frequently until finally her mother sought help. 'I do everything for her, I buy her clothes, I try to teach her how to do things properly, but she resents every suggestion I make. Whenever I advise her she flies into a rage, screaming that she is no longer a baby. The only time she is fit to live with is when she has her own way.' The counselor listened patiently and then suggested that she might be able to help her. At first she couldn't see that *she* needed help, she thought it was Mary who should be talked to, but she was desperate and agreed.

After first letting Mary's mother tell her story again, the counselor advised less rather than more restriction, and more rather than less freedom. She explained that, after all, the mother's tactics had failed and that an opposite approach could hardly be worse. It wasn't worse, of course; on the contrary it succeeded. Mary hadn't needed all that protection, all those suggestions. She had grown up more than her mother, still deeply feeling the loss of her husband, could bear to believe. And Mary, needing and wanting her own independence, failed to understand the deep emotion which made her mother try to hold her so close.

Understood as a manifestation of thwarted attempts at independence, adolescent rebellion is easier for a parent to tolerate. So, too, is it easier for them to sit by and see mistakes being made when they realize that mistakes made now mean fewer in the future. Young people's errors in choice of friends, their poor planning, their low grades in subjects parents could have helped them with, are hard to take, much harder than were the falls that accompanied those first halting steps; but parents need to realize that even as children learned to walk smoothly by letting them try, so will they become mature and able to protect themselves only by letting them do for themselves. It helps parents to understand this, and to loosen the reins, if some counselor—teacher, minister, doctor, no matter who it is, whom they respect—explains and listens and takes some of the responsibility for the new way of meeting the situation.

So much for how adults feel. How about young people themselves?

It does not always require much restraint to produce signs

of rebellion. These young people are less confident than they care to admit; their show of defiance is balanced precariously. Angrily protesting that they are no longer babies, they fear independence, shrink from it, and may tomorrow seek the very help they reject today. The more confused and anxious, the less confident they are, the more defiantly they behave. Lacking in confidence, they bolster it with the noise, if not the substance, of power. The not answering, the slammed doors, the not talking, the shouting are rude—but they are much more than rudeness. They are ways of saying, 'I want to be independent, I want to handle this myself—whenever you come into it, it's just that much less my own.' As Bill groped toward independence, he seemed ruthlessly to reject his parents and to deny the value of all his parents' ideas and plans. He appeared to want to abandon those people to whom he had been so closely tied in his early years. It was as if, in order to help himself to break those close ties, he felt compelled to voice his low opinion of his parents and their ideas. Finding this break very difficult, to deny vociferously the worth of all he had loved and accepted made it easier for him.

Ironically, those adolescents who find the leaving of their parents and the acquisition of independence most difficult treat their parents the most cruelly: the more breaking away disturbs a boy or girl, the more fierce and childish will be the outbursts. The boy who swears at his mother, refuses to study, spits at his sister, slams doors, acts sullen, and comes to the table late, unwashed, is not just rude and nasty and impossible. He is confused; he wants independence, yet fears it; and when he finally strives for it, he is thwarted. So, too, the girl who 'won't listen,' who insists on behaving the way she says other girls do, who won't help around the house, stays out late, mimics much older girls in dress and habits, and considers her parents old-fashioned. Confused and frustrated, they become at times frantic, and then like all frantic people they revert to unreasoning, impetuous violent behavior.

Nothing is of more importance to an adolescent's development than the manner in which inevitable conflicts are settled. 'I haven't time to explain, do as I say' should be reserved for such times as when the house is on fire. 'Get in at ten tonight, and I don't want any discussion about it' may get you back to your newspaper, but it hardly establishes communication. A willingness to listen to the other side, to put yourself in his place, teaches by example the sort of interpersonal relationships which would make this world a better place for all of us. But not to be in control, to refuse to guide the family or school or club, to leave young people entirely to their own whims and interests, breeds insecurity and anxiety. Until they're ready to ship out alone, they need to feel that the helm is in strong, capable hands.

Fear of responsibility, a preference for dependence, an apparent reluctance to enter womanhood or manhood, a failure to struggle against too-tight reins—those are a more disheartening spectacle than is defiance. The spiritless boy or girl accepting oversolicitude and domination is relinquishing the remaining hope of independence.

Where there is dependence, the scene in school or at home is quieter, but the future is more forbidding. Phil's mother couldn't understand that. And later she couldn't understand his failure in his senior year in high school. She had, as she put it, 'done everything for him.' Not being allowed to do for himself, it was inevitable that he either remain totally dependent or that he become resentful. Phil's marks were failing. He was fed up with school, but he had no thought of doing anything but dragging along. During his grade school years he had done very well, and there was no reason to doubt his ability. He talked freely about his mother, of her boundless energy and the efficient way she handled things both at home and in his father's business. But it was not her dominance and overprotection which was most disturbing: it was Phil's failure to rebel. Dependent and irresponsible by nature, neither independence nor responsibility had been fostered by others and now was not being sought by the boy himself. His school thought him 'such a nice boy—perhaps a little lazy, but he'll grow out of it. He's no real trouble at all—not like some of our boys.'

Conformity and docility, which make for 'low nuisance value' in the classroom and home, strike fear in the hearts of those who want democracy and a free culture to survive. The orderliness and discipline of the ant world must often have seemed heaven to a harassed parent or weary teacher, but excessive conformity stifles the progress that the free play of individuality permits. Neither wanton individualism nor selfish aggression is commendable in the individual or the state; but its opposite, because its undermining influence is so subtle, too seldom worries us. Few of us think the status quo perfect, but many of us resent and thwart and fear those independent individuals who would try to change the shape of things for the better. We condemn and we fear agitators, but we are endangered as much by those who passively submit and who withdraw from responsibility.

Rebelliousness needs to be properly channeled, not condemned: independence and the fruits of individuality need to be cherished. It is no less imperative that the extremes of conformity and dependence be given attention and that when found they be startled out of 'their obsequious salute to power and to the status quo.' Judge Learned Hand once warned us eloquently: 'Our dangers, as it seems to me, are not from the outrageous but from the conforming; not from those who rarely and under the lurid glare of obloquy upset our moral complaisance, or shock us with unaccustomed conduct, but from those, the mass of us, who take their virtues and tastes, like their shirts and their furniture, from the limited patterns which the market offers . . . all confidently assured that nothing was lacking to their complete realization of the Human Ideal. Over that chorus the small voice of the individual sounds not even the thinnest obligato; it seems senseless and preposterous to sing at all . . . Our problem, as I see it, is how to give the mannikin, assailed on all hands with what we now so like to call propaganda, the chance of survival as a person at all, not merely as a leaf driven by the wind, a symbol in a formula.'

Adolescents thrive on responsibility—the more you give them, the better they learn to handle it. It is only when too much is expected of them without any preparation, or when responsibility is too long withheld and then thrown at them all at once, that they are apt to fail. Rebellion is a straining at the bit; it is solved by loosening, not by tightening the reins.

If young people are to develop into mature, independent, self-reliant men and women capable of respect for authority and for the rights and needs of others, they must be given ever-increasing opportunities to venture. They need to put meaning into those personalities which love and security gave so fine an early start. That beginning was only a preparation for living. In adolescence they need to practice living like the adults they are beginning to be. As they grow they must learn to protect themselves, to develop their own attitudes and interests, their own personalities. When they have done this, they will be ready for *interdependent*, not independent, truly mature living in a cooperative and peaceful world. If we continue to run their lives, continue to protect them, we can only leave them without protection, without confidence in themselves, and without minds of their own.

5

WAYS TO HELP
ADOLESCENTS

The adult who is aware of an adolescent's emotional problem early in its development is in a position to be of inestimable help. Many of the emotional difficulties of adolescents, if caught soon enough, can be resolved in a very short time. This is no exaggeration. When a student is given help early in the course of his emotional upset, a brief talk, lasting perhaps no more than fifteen minutes, may be sufficient to explain the nature of his problem to him and enable him to cope with it. When offered early, attentive and active listening—that is, listening that can construe the adolescent groping for appropriate words to describe his distress, and the finding of those words, or the offering of them by the listener—can clarify a confusing situation and quickly dissipate it.

Parents, teachers, club leaders, and coaches are in an unusually strategic position to detect the first signs of a developing problem. Recognition of these signs depends to a considerable extent upon a close and continuous relationship: under such conditions a change in behavior is usually noted. However, at times familiarity seems to dull perception, and a stranger may immediately consider behavior unusual which an adolescent's close associates at home, in school, in clubs, or at church have failed to notice. Parents, nevertheless, are usually the first to observe a change in the behavior of a son or daughter. A previously lively and happy boy or girl whose school marks fall off abruptly for no obvious reason, who becomes unusually quiet and withdrawn, rebellious, sad, nervous, or seems unable to concentrate or get to sleep, or who seems preoccupied, deserves attention. This is not to say that all such young people have problems, or that all of those who do cannot solve them themselves, but it is to say that these signs should not be ignored.

The adult who is going to help adolescents needs more than the ability to recognize early signs. His response to them is of paramount importance. For instance, the adult faced with an angry and upset adolescent may become defensive, feeling that the anger is in part directed toward himself as a representative of the older generation. With his attitude colored by feelings of this kind he will have little success. The listener must be able to abandon for a time his identification with the older generation and must attempt to see the problem through the adolescent's eyes. Since all of us regress every night in our dreams, it should not be impossible to regress sufficiently so that we can adopt the adolescent's point of view. Then, appraising his problem from this viewpoint, we can examine it and use whatever wisdom we have acquired as adults.

Some listeners are rendered ineffective because they are unconsciously moved by desires for control or power. They cannot wait to talk, to advise, to criticize; they seem unable to relax and to nod as a friend would do. The attempt to control, the attempt to order, admonish, or direct, is one of the most damaging of tendencies for those who would help an adolescent. It can only call forth the same rebellious response that the adolescent had been making for a considerable period before he sought help. Adolescents have had years of listening, years of hearing what parents, teachers, society, and the books say. Their doubts, their feelings, their questions, and their opinions yearn for expression. They have had a surfeit of listening—now they want and need to talk. Often a parent who wants to tell a boy's story for him will say, 'Well, talk to him if you want to, but you won't get anything out of him. He never says anything.' When a good listener hears such a remark, he instinctively plans to allow at least an hour for his visit with the boy. The trouble will not be how to get him to talk but how to find time enough to listen to all he wants, and needs, to say.

Conversation is of course more than just listening; but listening is so much more effective than preaching, and the boy's telling you is much more valuable than your telling him, that its importance cannot be overemphasized. To have him put his thoughts and feelings into words is all-important: what he says is secondary. The *feeling* he puts into his words is what counts. You should be reluctant to advise or to tell him about yourself. What to ask, what to say, when to say nothing, are things one gradually learns.

Some adults who seem to wish to help disturbed adolescents unconsciously picture themselves as a kind of protector or nurturer, a motherly figure who shields and supports the shorn lambs. These, too, usually fail to establish an effective relationship. In fact, they may arouse such intense anxiety in the adolescent that he will beat a hasty retreat.

On the other hand, granted the ability to see things through young people's eyes, and freedom from such motivations as those just mentioned, listening can be much more effective than many adults realize. Listening, however, is much more than just not talking. James Stephens defined a good listener as 'one who likes the person who is talking' and added, 'No person, however gifted, is talking at his best unless he likes the people he is talking to, and knows that they like him.'

Furthermore, listening is an art: it is active, not passive. It requires the listener to be alert at all times to the play of feelings that goes on when two people, one of whom is upset, talk together. Since many adolescents are in the process of acquiring an active, dynamic vocabulary, it is often necessary, for example, to suggest in a tentative fashion a word that may be suitable to describe the emotion they are groping and struggling to express. At such a time the choice of the right single word will act as a catalyst and crystallize the entire thought and feeling around the problem. Subsequently, the change for the better in the boy's or girl's demeanor may be far beyond what might have been expected.

Listening to an adolescent, though an active rather than a passive process, often calls for silence. When an adolescent really lets his words flow and his feelings go, this is the time to remain silent. Any comment or suggestion should be held in reserve; no more than an occasional monosyllable or nod of approval or recognition is called for. Later, when the adolescent's stream of thought and feeling begins to dry up, is the time for the listener to prevent the growth of an undesirable degree of emotional tension which a long period of silence might cause. Rather than let silence persist to that point almost any friendly comment will do. It may be that the material the adolescent had been discussing can furnish a word or phrase which, when repeated by the listener, will enable him to resume talking. At other times it will be worthwhile to change the subject entirely in order to give him a rest from the emotional strain his outburst may have caused him. Everything said in the initial talk should be designed to increase the adolescent's approval and acceptance of the listener, and to establish a warm and friendly relationship.

A notable exception to this is the younger adolescent of, say, eleven to fourteen, who lacks verbal facility. Young people vary in the age at which they acquire an active vocabulary that permits them freely to express themselves. All through their childhood they amass an ever increasing vocabulary of static words, that is to say, words which have meaning for them, but which they are unable to use readily in ordinary conversation. Early adolescence is the time when the process of changing this large static vocabulary to a dynamic one goes on. During this period, words which were always understood now gradually become ones with meaning *for them*, and therefore ones they can now use to express their own feelings and emotional needs. Consequently, with the younger, the less verbal, adolescents, the technique of getting them to talk in a meaningful fashion will differ. We must be prepared to offer a word as a possible solution whenever the adolescent flounders or gropes for the right one. If our choice of word is successful, the young adolescent will grasp it avidly and, seeing how completely it describes the feelings with which he is grappling, will use it again and again. It will, as it were, have been promoted to membership in his dynamic vocabulary.

Furthermore, with these less verbal adolescents, the silent periods should be extremely brief. At this age, feelings of hostility and rebellion run very high, and an adult's silence is likely to mobilize and increase the adolescent's anxiety to the point that he will refuse to return for further talks. Alertness, imagination, and resourcefulness in perceiving the direction in which the young adolescent's thought and feeling are struggling *and* in suggesting words that will help him to express his emotions are essential if we are to give these less verbal people the most effective help.

It must be borne in mind that in the communication between an adult and an adolescent there are many elements supplementing the verbal exchange. These nonverbal cues are present in every conversation, but they have become so automatic that we are rarely conscious of using them. However, different, fleeting, and infinitely varied movements of the facial muscles, the expression in the eyes, the tone of the voice, the tilt of the head, the use of the hands, the position of the legs and trunk, all can have important meanings. Look for them, and learn from them some of the matters that the boy or girl may not be putting into words. Furthermore, be aware that your own mannerisms and facial expressions are communicating information about you.

Disordered feeling or emotion is the basis of all neurotic disturbance. In the neuroses the emotions appear to have been upset because the sufferer has never put into words his fears and hatreds and loves. When these have neither been relieved nor expressed verbally, they must find another outlet for expression; and so, instead of losing their force in speech, they flow out through one of the outlets of the nervous system, whose language is headache, indigestion, diarrhea, backache, or one or another of a host of bodily symptoms. A careful diagnostic search will fail to reveal any tangible basis for these headaches, backaches, or other symptoms, but they are no less uncomfortable and real, although their origin is emotional. Vomiting because your school or sister or boss makes you sick is just as real as the vomiting which results from infection. Unfortunately the expression of one's emotions by way of the nervous system is no more than a bodily symptom; it gives no lasting relief. This type of expression is only *evidence* of the repressed emotions; it is *not a satisfactory outlet* for them.

These feelings must be put into words if they are really to be relieved and their threat to physical and mental health overcome. So the primary goal of the treatment of a neurosis is no more and no less than to put these feelings into words and thereby achieve an understanding of their nature and of their relationship to the present symptoms and behavior. When this is done, energy will no longer be used to repress these confused and powerful feelings and they will no longer need to be expressed as symptoms through the nervous system.

These psychosomatic symptoms will be discussed in more detail in another chapter. Here we wish only to indicate how a knowledge of their origin and causes can profitably be used in the classroom and the youth group for the purpose of preventing their manifestation. Exercises which freely use speech such as student dramatics, discussions, and debates have tremendous value for young people's mental health.

Opportunities given the adolescent to express his own feelings are often meager. Those few are further limited by the relative inability of many adolescents to express themselves in speech. This inability may well contribute to their need to *act out* their feelings. When youngsters drive recklessly we may well ask ourselves 'What are they trying to *say* by this behavior?' The chances are that most of them are trying to say several things at once. Boys, especially, are trying to say, 'See how unlike my mother I am! I'm brave and daring and tough and all male!' Girls, on the other hand, may be trying to say, 'Even though I'm not a man, I can take it as well as they can!' Were they able to express these attitudes in words—and to understand them— their need to act them out could be much reduced.

By giving adolescents every acceptable opportunity to express feelings clamoring to be relieved, their emotional health

will be safeguarded, and yet there need be little interference
with the group or school program. Those schools where the
teacher acts as a listener, encouraging spontaneous comments
from the students in open classroom discussion, debates, and
dramatics, are found to be producing very desirable changes in
young people's behavior. Topics should be chosen which will
encourage thinking and feeling in areas of strong emotion so
that students are led to talk about their fears, hatreds, and loves.

This sort of classroom technique does not produce young
brave-new-world creatures. On the contrary it promotes the development of every pupil's individuality. Nor will it, as some
adults fear, destroy those forces which push one on into truly
great creative work. There is little basis in fact for the opinion
that by freeing people of their hates and fears, they will lose the
source of their creativity. Creative power lies not in the tortured
areas of a man's being, but in the force for life and creation that
seeks to push outward to expression. The objective is to clear
the inner channels in a boy or girl so that this force will be able
to flow out with as little impediment as possible. Many creative
artists experience phases when they accomplish much and
periods of little accomplishment and discouragement; but once
having rid themselves of the inner blocks to their own creative
forces, such artists may be expected to reach high levels of activity which they can sustain for much longer periods.

The importance of the spoken word to mental health must
not be confused with other types of expression. Other means of
expression can serve as outlets for those feelings that are not
widely accepted by society. In the graphic arts, for example,
feelings that would be censured if written or spoken can be ac-
ceptably expressed in sculpture and painting. Music, as Edward
Hitschmann pointed out, is the most effective of all the arts in
expressing feelings which society would not tolerate if expressed
in words. But although the arts provide channels for the relief of

inner tension, they are not a complete substitute for the spoken word. They fail to increase one's self-awareness and self-acceptance. It is not enough to express feeling: one must understand these feelings and their relationships to one's thoughts and behavior.

Nor are such activities as the dance or athletics, which provide splendid outlets for aggressive impulses, as effective in promoting emotional stability and maturity as is speech. These activities are comparable to what is called acting out in the treatment of emotional disorders. In acting out, the patient regresses to childlike action to express impulses he is unable to put into words. The boy who smashes his schoolroom window or hurls chalk at his blackboard is saying by his actions things which are too violent for him to say in words.

When encouraged, speaking out one's feelings will do much for young people's mental health. It is obviously well within the power of any teacher or group leader and the scope of any curriculum to furnish many such opportunities. The rewards for all concerned will be rich. To the boy or girl will come poise and inner security and progress toward emotional maturity, and to the teacher will come new insights into his own personality and a heightened awareness of the meaning of his students' and friends' behavior.

When dealing with early, middle, or late adolescence the most important procedure of all is the establishment of a positive relationship. This involves a transference of the adolescent's childhood attitudes or emotional habits of love and admiration toward his parents to the listener, and constitutes the most powerful lever in helping an adolescent with his emotional problems.

It is important to stress that transference in adolescence differs from the type that occurs in either childhood or adult life, for it is not restricted to the parents or members of the immediate family, nor does it have the neurotic quality encountered in some adults.

You have only to go to any ballfield to find young adolescents copying, in all their ways of fielding and throwing and batting, the stances, movements, and attitudes of big league baseball players. This kind of imitative behavior is one of the cardinal characteristics of transference in adolescence. It is therefore not surprising that adolescents, particularly the older ones who have been floundering, suddenly decide to become doctors or counselors, or coaches or teachers, in imitation of the person who at that point has had the understanding to listen to them and so help them order the emotional forces with which they have been struggling.

Once this positive relationship, this transference, has been established, the succeeding talks will provide opportunities for giving help in a variety of ways. It is remarkable how quickly many adolescents develop insight into the nature of their emotional difficulties. It may be that the normal fluidity of an adolescent's feelings makes his unconscious readily accessible: the conflicts of adolescents appear to be less deeply repressed than those of adults, and it appears to be possible for them to recognize and accept unconscious impulses and to relate them to their personality and life experience in such a way that true insight develops without the interference of defensive intellectualization.

One serious word of caution is necessary at this point. Everyone who deals with adolescent boys and girls should be alert to the possibility that he himself may become too involved with the young person he is trying to help. Just as the adolescent develops strong emotional ties to his sympathetic listener, so, too, may this adult develop close emotional ties to the adolescent. This emotional reaction in the adult is referred to as *countertransference*. Feelings of this kind represent the awakening of the same habits of relating emotionally toward this adolescent that have been used since childhood toward various other people.

On the other hand, there is much unnecessary concern in the minds of teachers and other advisers. These people, who clearly can be very helpful to many adolescents, often feel themselves to be amateurs and fear doing irreparable harm. It would seem well to keep in mind that people have been confiding in one another without the analytic couch or consultation room for thousands of years.

The whole realm of semantics and communication between individuals is so rich and so vast that any well-intentioned person can be assured that if he or she be willing to listen patiently to any adolescent who shows a wish to talk, they will be serving this adolescent in a way in which parents often cannot. Physicians, ministers, teachers, advisers, all people who have to deal intimately with the adolescent, are in a highly strategic position to encourage the outpourings of confused, frustrated, and angry youngsters. They are seeking recognition, support, direction, and trust from the older generation, but of a different nature from that they have received from their parents and relatives through the years. It must be remembered that it is not easy for parents (who as they grow older tend to become increasingly rigid in their attitudes toward their children) to accept an adolescent with his or her dawning maturity as a young adult. They say—or think: 'Well, he may be fourteen, but he's still my little boy.' And we can be sure that the boy or girl responds as savagely to that type of comment or attitude as we would expect. Therefore, any adult who deals with adolescents is in a position to render them great service in their struggle to mature. Needless to say, it is extremely helpful if such a person has available as his mentor, guide, or consultant a person with professional training to whom he can turn when something puzzling or frustrating turns up. Such help can be invaluable, but the actual dealing with the adolescent is the most valuable experience of all. The business of counseling is an art, and, like all arts, it must be practiced to be learned. The best, clearest, and most elaborately formulated rules will desert a person in the rapid give-and-take of a conversation: one must learn its art the way one learns any art in which timing is a crucial factor.

Occasionally, in dealing with an adolescent's emotional problem, one flash of insight is sufficient to change the whole balance of emotional forces within him, and greatly change his behavior and life direction. A case in point is that of a young man who had one of the most common of adolescents' problems, worry over masturbation. His job was one not highly differentiated from a masculine-feminine point of view, and it was evident that his choice of this career had been influenced in part by his still unresolved attachment to his mother. This also seemed to be a considerable factor in the compulsive masturbation which caused him so much distress. In the course of his second talk, he brought out more and more clearly how his interests and leanings paralleled very closely those of his mother, and that his sister, a year or two younger than he, had all the interests and attributes of his father. The number of parallels between himself and his mother, and between his sister and his father, were so obvious that it suddenly struck him that this degree of coincidence went far beyond what might be considered normal. It was suggested to him at this point that it would seem that his mother's feminine influence over him might well be creating a considerable degree of tension: after all, he was a male and could not possibly hope to be a female like his mother. This observation was made toward the end of the talk.

A week later, a changed young man presented himself. He had been out to his first dance and had taken out three different girls. At this visit he also talked in an aggressive fashion for the first time. He told how he had gone out for the track team and was enjoying it, and that he was now dispatching his homework with efficiency. He was obviously a very different person.

A maneuver that occasionally is effective is to confront the adolescent directly and bluntly with the true meaning of his behavior, that is, what it is accomplishing for him. This will often proceed in a natural way out of encouraging him to voice his thoughts and feelings. After he has brought out a number of factors that are obviously related, you confront him with their multiple relationships. Confronting him with such a summation of evidence will sharpen his focus on his behavior and various attitudes, and can contribute to his developing insight. One boy, a high-school sophomore, had been doing poorly academically, socially, and in athletics. He also had a history of staying out of school for little reason during most of his entire seventh-grade year. He complained about his school's facilities, teaching, and about his coaches and fellow students. When confronted with the obvious, 'You've always had trouble making friends, haven't you?' he abandoned his evasiveness and became willing and able to accept help with his real problem.

Though it is often helpful to explain to the adolescent what the nature of his struggle may be, this explanation must be approached thoughtfully and the words carefully chosen. The wrong words may have little impact: against certain ones many of us have built up intellectual defenses. For example, while the Oedipus complex is now widely understood, it almost inevitably evokes an intellectual defense, because it has been stripped of all emotion. Use of some simple, earthy, strong expression, such as 'all wrapped up in your mother,' is much more likely to bring an adolescent to a realization of his situation. The same boy might glibly handle 'Oedipus complex' with complete emotional detachment.

Another matter relevant to the question of techniques to use with upset adolescents is the way in which different personalities think and express themselves. Some adolescents have minds that think in words. These highly verbal young people are in many instances heavily armed with intellectual defenses. When this is the case, it must be recognized and attempts made to get the adolescent to use a less sophisticated vocabulary. What we want, what will benefit him, is for him to express himself *with feeling*. Simple, earthy words do this, not polite, fancy, evasive ones.

Other adolescents, perhaps very gifted, tend to think in pictures. When you encounter this type of thinking, it is essential to have great patience and, also, to reassure them that there is no hurry. Make it clear that you want them to take their time and to describe the various pictorial ideas that occur to them.

Still others are gifted in nonverbal and nonpictorial thinking modalities. These may be the musicians and the mathematicians, and for them expressing thought and feeling in words is a difficult task. Here again, patience is required. Primarily, however, we need to recognize that we may have need for recourse to the same kinds of maneuvers employed with the very young, and therefore the less verbal, adolescent. At such times we need to be on the alert for the direction of the adolescent's thoughts and feelings, so that we can offer him words that carry emotional weight and may be suitable vehicles for them.

It is obvious that there are a number of other ways in which the adolescent can be helped in addition to the ways that have been described: these have been emphasized because of their primary importance. Other methods include the manipulation of the environment, the type of support that anyone would give to a friend in trouble, reassurance, the expression of hope, the clear indication of an alliance with the adolescent in his struggles with his problem, direct advice when it is asked for, and last, but not least, praise.

A frantic adolescent may request direct advice: your hesitation then to give it will only increase his anxiety and destroy his hope that you would help him. At other times advice is best given tangentially, in this fashion: 'You know, Bill, I talked with a fellow a couple of years ago who had very much the same problem you have. He tried an approach which I'll tell you about: it solved his problem. We might talk this over, and see if you think it is worth trying.' This indirect style obviates your appearing to have adopted a parentlike form of pressure and preserves the independent position of the adolescent. Given this freedom, an adolescent will often do the very thing suggested, feeling that he is doing so without having yielded to authoritarianism.

Much can be accomplished by enabling the parents to talk with a competent person. Under some circumstances this can be the same adult who is helping their son or daughter, but it is frequently preferable that this be another person. One of the most common sources of an adolescent's difficulties lies in his rebellion; consequently your dealing with his parents may arouse suspicion or a feeling that you also are on the adults' side. The degree to which this is a factor must be determined in each instance. It is a matter which can be overemphasized, but it should never be disregarded. Except in a real emergency, you should have no communication with other people concerning any adolescent you are attempting to help, without his knowledge.

At times a situation can be modified in such a way that a positive benefit will accrue. When, for instance, a boy or girl is in a school where conditions are definitely unfavorable, a change in schools may bring about a major change in academic performance. Similarly, relieving them of excessive obligations—such as a job too time-consuming or involvement in too much athletics or too many extracurricular activities—may be of considerable help.

At all times it is important to bear in mind that one is dealing with an individual, and to try to discover in the background of his life activity the factors that may be influencing him or her in such a way that emotional efficiency is impaired. A careful scrutiny of an individual's daily patterns of activity may reveal an obvious factor that was previously overlooked.

Sympathetic listening can be an important treatment tool and should, as a matter of fact, be used at the beginning of every form of treatment, but at times a more sophisticated approach will be required.

During the past few years significant progress has been made in the treatment of emotional disorders. For example, the basic findings and theories of psychoanalysis have been refined and adapted for use in various forms of brief psychotherapy, and the progress in the study of dreaming (REM—rapid eye movement brain waves, et cetera) have opened new approaches to the use of the dream in treatment.

For the adolescent with psychosomatic or other emotional disorders the use of the dream can be therapeutic. It becomes prophylactic as the recounting of remembered dreams helps the maturing adolescent to become familiar with the universal language of the dream and so to add new depth and breadth to his or her vocabulary.

As a result of dream study, a strong emotional tie develops between the listener and the adolescent that inspires in the adolescent confidence in the listener and a readiness to trust him with the most intimate details of his thoughts and feelings. Equipped with words which are highly charged with feeling, he can express hitherto pent-up emotion. The relief which follows can often so change the balance of forces in the adolescent that it alone will suffice to correct what may have seemed to have been an almost insoluble problem.

There is present, too, in most adolescents, a strong need to find a hero or heroine upon which to model their own conduct. As a part of accomplishing the tasks of adolescence, the finding of a suitable model of the same sex to copy helps the adolescent to develop and define his or her own ego and its boundaries. It is, in fact, a part of the developing independence from the immediate family.

The act of telling your dreams to another trusted person— i.e. the sharing of intimate material—contributes to the development of a therapeutically valuable relationship between the adolescent and the listener. In technical language this relation is called 'transference,' a term coined by Freud who found that his patients inclined to behave toward him as they had behaved in childhood toward their own parents. He observed that they seemed to have 'transferred' to him, as therapist, the behavior patterns that they used originally in relating to their own parents in infancy and childhood.

With the development of 'transference feelings' toward the listener, a response on the latter's part also usually occurs. This response is called countertransference and embodies the same basic mechanisms that go on in the adolescent. If the listener is unaware of the possibility of this kind of feeling developing in himself, he (or she) may be drawn into a highly emotional relation with his troubled adolescent which could develop aspects extremely difficult for him and the adolescent.

Awareness of and anxiety about the emotional tensions encountered in the transference-countertransference situation has contributed to the reluctance of many ancillary workers to embark on any attempt to help the emotionally troubled adolescent. Yet the number of well-trained professionals is so scant and the number of adolescents so large that the use of any worthy listener should not be scorned. The help of every parent, teacher, coach, youth leader, clergyman, and sympathetic adult is needed. When we consider the masses of adolescents not attending school whose communication with the world around them is so meager, we gain some awareness of the extent of the great need.

A number of other treatment forms have been developed in recent years. These have been based for the most part upon the pioneer work of Pavlov some fifty years ago. Behavior therapy, for example, is a kind of treatment in which the sufferer is trained to endure increasing degrees of some stimulus which has caused excessively painful reaction often to a disabling extent. A series of scenes or situations are placed in a graded 'hierarchy' and the sufferer's tolerance for them modified by the use of relaxation exercises such as Jacobson's, or through Transcendental Meditation. If an adequate gradation of intensity of stimuli is arranged and the relaxation responses to them well established, relief from suffering is obtained in a relatively short time. Behavior therapy is of value in the treatment of phobias of various kinds and conditions in which the sufferer's responses to stimuli are out of all proportion to the nature of the stimulus.

Another new therapeutic modality is known as operant conditioning. This kind of treatment is more directly Pavlovian in nature. Both noxious stimuli and reward stimuli are used to condition the sufferer's responses. One of the simplest examples of this treatment form is the use of the drug Antabuse in the treatment of alcoholism. The medicine is taken in the morning and continued daily until a suitable level of the drug in the bloodstream is attained. Thereafter, the taking of alcohol in any form will produce extremely unpleasant symptoms, to avoid which the unstable alcoholic addict will stop drinking.

We have touched upon a few of the techniques we have

found rewarding in our efforts to help adolescents. No two young people are alike, so obviously what will help one adolescent may not be successful with another. As one gains experience in helping adolescents who have emotional difficulties, more and more methods will be discovered. However, the major prerequisites are the abilities to listen, to guide the conversation into productive channels, and to allow a useful relationship to form and to handle it objectively.

The serious disorders of feeling which appear in adolescence require psychotherapy. Clearly it is much more efficient to exert our energy to try to prevent these troubles. This can be done by all interested and discerning adults who are closely associated with adolescents. What is needed is sympathy, the will to help, a belief in the primary importance of mental health, and a knowledge of the elementary principles of mental hygiene. Given these, a parent, teacher, club leader, or other adult can play an important part in keeping these young people healthy in mind and more effective in their jobs and studies. When a school or club or home has good leadership, morale will be good. There will not be widespread undercurrents of anxiety and insecurity when there is a capable and respected hand at the helm, and there will not be outbursts of resentment and aggression when the leadership is strong but not arbitrary.

Finally, a few comments should be made about the feelings of some people that all adolescents should be treated with kid gloves lest a psychosis or suicide or homicide eventuate. That kind of tragedy follows only when an adolescent has a very severe emotional disorder. It has no relevance to the vast majority of upset adolescents temporarily bowled over by the common stresses associated with growing up. It is these youngsters who are likely to be encountered by the general practitioner, the pediatrician, the internist, the pastor, the youth leader, or the teacher. The others, the seriously ill, are obviously not his province: these, and any others about whom he has the slightest doubt, he should unhesitatingly refer to a psychiatrist.

Some adolescents—fortunately the percentage is small—do develop severe disorders, but a moderate amount of experience, common sense, and intelligence will enable anyone to distinguish these. The rule that we have suggested in a previous chapter still obtains. Any of these adults whom we have mentioned should have a few talks with the upset adolescent, not peremptorily reject him; but, if at the end of three of these visits this adult feels uneasy, or that no progress is being made, referral to a psychiatrist is indicated. After three interviews an adult familiar with young people will have a very good idea of whether he is dealing with someone he can help or someone whom he should refer.

6

ANXIETY STATES

Anxiety states are not as common in adolescents as in adults, but not a few will experience a period of anxiety which is at least temporarily upsetting. During this transition period some find it too difficult to adjust to their new feelings about sex and their relationships to their parents; seek independence; build up their own personalities and confidence by means of those achievements which bring recognition; and meet the confusions which school, religion, adults' behavior, death, career choice, and a host of other questions may pose. That all of these often constitute problems does not mean that most adolescents do not solve them quite adequately. Most do, and the period of handicapping confusion and worry is usually quite brief. However, for one reason or another, some problems are more troublesome for some adolescents than for others, and touch off the development of an 'anxiety state.' This is no more than to say that for the time being this young person's problems are more than he can handle: they, to a certain extent, are running *him*, are keeping him from working and living as happily and efficiently as he should.

Anxiety takes many forms. It may occur at a deep, unconscious level and be evidenced only by some symptom typical of physical illness, or it may appear close to the surface of consciousness in the form of those body responses which we associate with fear. A dry mouth, rapid breathing, fast heart rate, dilated pupils, 'gooseflesh,' a tight or sinking feeling in the stomach, and taut muscles are all part of a fear reaction. They indicate readiness to fight whatever has suddenly threatened, or to flee if the threat proves too great to overcome. Such a state of readiness cannot be maintained very long because our reserves of hormones and chemicals which produce it are small and quickly exhausted.

Man's mind has two parts: the conscious, where most external and internal activity goes on at a level which can be put into words; and the unconscious, where much that goes on is not put into words but where, because of the nature of its ties to the entire nervous system, its power to stir the body is great. An unknown sound, for example, may produce a different response in each of three listeners: a sound from a dark woods' path will suggest a wild beast to one, a dangerous snake to another, and a lost dog to a third. The first listener will take to his heels; the second will freeze to the spot to avoid being struck; and the third will only call out, 'Here, boy!' Each one will have the bodily feelings of fear, though of considerably varying degree and duration.

Anxiety, like fear, has its origin in something unknown, something mysterious. Not being known, whatever it is which we experience cannot be put into words; we don't know the sound, the shape, the event for what it really is so we can't call it by name or describe it in words. In short, we do not understand it. For instance, the adolescent, seeing his parents in conflict, may be mystified and anxious. It is upsetting to him, for the dependent little boy within him still *feels* and regards Father and Mother as his strong bulwark against the threats of the outside world. But now things are strange; his strong defenses have been lost and all that is left is uncertainty. Faced with the possibility of their divorce, he may perhaps feel triumphant for now he will have Mother all to himself; but this will quickly be erased by the feelings of disloyalty to his father, who has meant so much to him. In short he doesn't know where he stands; he doesn't understand; it is something unknown and mysterious—so he is *anxious*.

These conflicting emotions create a storm of feeling deep within him that cannot be fully resolved until he has expressed them in words and come to understand them. If they remain unresolved, at an unconscious and wordless level, they will seek and find some other outlet. They may drain energy from his conscious activity so that he will not concentrate on his studies and he may daydream and be unable to recall what he dreams about; or his conflict may be shunted into his nervous system and cause such symptoms as nausea, diarrhea, or headache. These are the things that are likely to happen if his feelings about this situation are not expressed, if he does not come to understand them.

Conflict between their parents and the attendant insecurity in their homes is but one of the many reasons for adolescents' anxiety. Poor progress in school, their sexual adjustment and unpopularity are frequently upsetting. Those whose childhood has permitted the development of independent and emotionally stable personalities take most of these matters in their stride. It is the dependent, insecure young people who are bowled over, and it is these we need to help to become more secure, more independent. Whatever can be done to foster this will obviously be of real preventive value.

Jim had always leaned heavily on his mother for protection. She helped him with his homework, she kept him from school when he ate little or no breakfast or when he said his stomach was upset, she shielded him from his father's sporadic attempts to 'make a man of him.' Nothing was too good for Jim. He had tutoring 'because he needed individual attention.' At that point he did! He had been helped so much that he couldn't help himself and it took the extra effort of several teachers to get him into college. He had a superficial charm, good manners, good looks, and more than enough intelligence to permit him to do very well in his studies. In college, however, he did miserably.

'They don't seem to take any personal interest in him, doctor. You have to understand Jim. He's lost weight and he doesn't eat well. I think something's worrying him.' It was. He was eating little, he had lost weight, and he had all manner of gastrointestinal symptoms. At first he offered one rationalization after another as the cause of his failure, but it was evident that the main trouble was simply that he had started off doing little or no studying and soon was far behind and in the sort of bind where only a more purposeful and independent boy could hope to prevail. Jim wasn't that sort; he just gave up. And then he began to worry about what might happen if he were to flunk out. How would his mother feel; what would his father do; what would his friends think? Casting among these thoughts, he neither faced his fundamental problem nor worked out his present one; and from week to week his anxiety increased. His dilemma was more than he could stand. He became panicky, lost his appetite, and began to have 'stomach trouble.' 'Stomach trouble' had been his means of getting out of school when he was a little boy, and now he could rely on it to get him out of college before he was 'fired.'

His stomach trouble firmly established as a means of handling his conflict and as an escape from school and from flunking out, it was difficult for him to allow himself to see his symptoms for what they were. It was even more of a task to try to strengthen his personality so that he would have more than symptoms of illness to call upon when a problem faced him. Here was a boy for whom so much had been done that he had had little ability to do for himself, a boy who had little confidence in himself; 'after all, no one thinks I can do anything, if they did they'd let me try.' Still dependent at an age when he should have been able not only to do for himself but to help others, he had neither the confidence nor the ability to work himself out of his difficulties.

The importance of letting young people do more and more for themselves and of showing them in this way your confidence in them are things we all have to remember. We are so sure we could do it better, that they could do better with our help, that if we don't help they will fail or be hurt, that we deprive them of the experiences that would increase both their confidence and their skill. No one would think of allowing young people to attempt too much too soon, but provided they are started very young and then given more and more and greater and greater opportunities to do for themselves, the dangers or mistakes which might result from an adult's failure to help them will be few. Their few errors and bumps will be better for them than to have come through unscathed with our help: the failure will not diminish their confidence, for they will be aware of our confidence in their ability to rise above occasional setbacks.

For Molly, aged seventeen, her 'I'm all mixed up' was only too obvious and clearly much more significant than the 'nervous stomach' which she had at first said was her problem.

At various times all through her life she had been bothered by what she called a 'nervous stomach.' When she started off in the first grade, food 'gagged' her. The next summer when her father insisted that she take swimming lessons (he had almost drowned the year before and now refused to go near the water) her stomach acted up again. When she was seven years old her mother died.

All through school she found it impossible to eat when examinations were due, and during her first month away at college she 'couldn't eat a thing.' She had never stopped to think that all these upsets were due to anxiety, but in talking about them she remembered things that had made these times more frightening than they usually would have been: her older sister's tales of what they do at school to little girls who don't behave, her father's near drowning, her father's stern and frequent reminders that college was a luxury and 'it wasn't my idea anyway' and 'you'd better do well or you'll come home.'

What was it that was frightening Molly now? 'Well, I might as well get it over with—I haven't been able to talk to anyone, I'm so mixed up I don't know where to start. It's this man . . .' Ever since she had been a little girl she had adored her father, despite his gruffness and rebuffs. She wanted to be like him—or perhaps like her older brother. Parties and dates were a waste of time. When she began to mature she had severe pains with her periods—'I don't know why; I didn't want to get out of anything; as a matter of fact it made me mad that I had them.' All through high school she went to every athletic event but not on a single date. Attractive, she was invited frequently at first but soon boys stopped trying.

And then, in her second year of college, it happened. 'He's not like those college boys who come up every weekend. He's more like my father. Yes, he's a good deal older than I am but that isn't important to me, though some of my friends keep harping on it. But I'm not sure. I like him, but I don't think I want to marry him; I don't think I want to marry anyone. He's nice to me and I don't want to hurt his feelings. I just can't make up my mind. *It makes me sick* to think about it, and it's got my father so upset that I avoid saying anything.'

Some apparently are little troubled by the loss of a parent, by threats of the dire things that may happen, or by frightening experiences. But many are, and those who are so constituted may find it difficult to manage these together with such matters as adjusting their feelings toward the parent of the opposite sex. For adults to be aware of these factors in young people's development is the first step toward helping them: the next is to see that they have the appropriate sort of adult friends. Anxious, confused, and unable to untangle her mixed feelings and fears, the whole situation had become more than Molly could '*stomach.*' She needed an opportunity to talk out these feelings of hers, and she needed professional help in understanding them and herself; and while she was doing this and developing more mature attitudes she needed sympathetic support.

Relief from anxiety requires that boys or girls put their upsetting feelings into their own words. When this has been done they will gradually be able to understand what has been going on within themselves and will be able to make a conscious decision regarding their conflict. This is not only a therapeutic but also a maturing experience, for in contrast to their conflicting feelings, it belongs in the adult world: it is an adult rather than a childish way of meeting a problem. In their early years individuals do not put their feelings into words; they cry and strike out against whatever seems hostile or unknown. It is only with maturity that feeling is transferred from thoughtless action into words and understanding. Now these feelings, and the conflicts they threaten to arouse, are no longer met with irresolution, and the adolescent is no longer torn between siding with either mother or father; no longer will the boy or girl fear condemnation and retribution from the one they reject; no longer do they fear growing up or assuming an adult's responsibilities. Whatever the outcome, their anxiety, since there is no longer an unknown and nameless conflict within them, will be largely resolved.

But by giving names to phenomena, we too often pretend to have solved their mystery. The different forms of anxiety are a case in point. There is so much to learn about them that each has been given a name. *Phobia* is one of these. It is, of course, no more than the Greek word for *fear*, and when it is better understood perhaps this classical name will be discarded and it may be called *unreasoning fear*, for such it is. It often has an element of anger too. When, for instance, a schoolboy's fear of an examination is entirely unreasonable and unjustified, what appears to be fear may in reality be anger.

Tom sought help because he invariably vomited on getting up in the morning on days when quizzes or examinations were scheduled. During an exam he would shake and sweat copiously; his thinking would be confused. Though well prepared, he usually failed miserably.

When he was encouraged to talk about his difficulty he was at first unable to say anything about it except to describe his symptoms. Later, as he continued to talk, he said that in an examination he had the feeling that he was a criminal who was being tried by a judge. Tom knew that he felt guilty about something but what it was he could not say at first. He said that he had felt much the same in coming for help, and he openly expressed feelings of anger and resentment toward his doctor. That he should feel this way baffled him until he realized that his family doctor reminded him of one of his teachers and, more significantly, of his father.

Once Tom had started to talk about his father it was as if a long and violent outpouring of anger had been released. He told how his father had 'deserted' him and his mother when he was eleven, and how before this his relationship to his father had been a long series of unfulfilled hopes and broken promises. Later it was suggested to him that his feeling of guilt in examinations might be due to his own dim awareness of the unfairness of his being angry at his blameless teacher, who not only was *not* his father but also differed considerably from him. Tom accepted this suggestion with great relief: he had bottled up his anger and resentment, and now that he had at long last put his feelings into words his symptoms gradually decreased.

Not all the upsets which examinations bring are related to fear of the tests themselves. School is an emotion-charged situation, where not infrequently teachers are associated in their pupils' minds with other adults whom they may either admire or dislike. Often these feelings have little apparent effect, but for some adolescents they may be the factor which determines success or failure. The important things to remember are that such feelings do exist, that in the classroom there is not just an intellectual but also an emotional interchange. At times a good relationship with a teacher results in a mediocre student's exceptional success, whereas a poor relationship may account for an excellent mind's inefficiency at school.

The tension which anxiety produces commonly causes boys and girls to forget the material they have studied for an examination. Amnesia is like this: it is just a more severe form of forgetting. A boy or girl who has amnesia may forget his own name and whereabouts, and may go away from home as if escaping some dreadful threat. He is in fact doing just that, except that what he fears and is trying to escape is within himself. When such a flight is as unfounded in reason as is a phobia, it is called a fugue.

To understand the nature of amnesia, it is necessary to remember the changes in feeling that occur during adolescence. In addition to a return to a state of self-love and preoccupation with himself, the adolescent boy is in the throes of diminution of his urges to be like his mother, of heightening his masculine behavior, and of rebelling against his father. The adolescent girl is relinquishing her tomboyishness, is breaking from her father, and is becoming increasingly feminine. These changes are not always easily or smoothly achieved. New feelings bring new responsibilities; the severing of old ties and the development of new ones are not painless.

For some adolescents changes in their feelings can be very confusing, and when there is another complicating factor, amnesia may be the result. It is as though the situation was so intolerable that to forget everything seems to be the only way out. Amnesia may develop, for instance, if a boy has developed an intense attachment for another boy or teacher or club leader. The homosexual cast of such a relationship excites intense anxiety. In the midst of trying to adjust to the usual changes in feeling which occur during these years, this boy is faced with the impossible task of understanding feelings which stem from self-love, from what is left of his desire to be feminine like his mother, from the attraction for whatever of the feminine exists in the boy or teacher or club leader, and in part from the masculine part of his own nature.

Bill was a personable eighteen-year-old when he was thrown into the exciting experience of college life as a freshman. He had been, as an only child, close to his father and even closer to his mother but had not, to all outward appearances, adopted any of her feminine traits. In the highly masculine atmosphere of the college dorm he found himself very much drawn to the companionship of one other boy. Their friendship, which at first started on a superficial level, gradually deepened until Bill became so powerfully involved in his fondness for his classmate that he began to be deeply upset. The nature of this disturbance was not apparent to Bill and only showed itself by an inability to sleep as soundly as he had formerly, a loss of interest in food, and considerable impairment in his powers of concentration and thinking.

One evening Bill disappeared. When he was picked up three days later in another city, quite unkempt, he had no recollection of what he had done in the intervening time and was completely bewildered by the whole affair. His parents and the school authorities had been very much troubled by this episode—a typical hysterical fugue, initiated by the intensity of the friendship between Bill and his classmate.

Once put into words, every tension growing out of incomprehensible feelings or situations too difficult for the person to solve loses its power to confuse or to necessitate such an escape as amnesia or fugue. To prevent the development of such tensions, one thinks of the importance of wider friendships rather than an excessively close attachment to a single member of one's own sex, the value of activities which widen one's circle of acquaintances and bring satisfaction and recognition, and the need for all of us to be more aware of the mechanisms of these difficulties so that we may earlier get at their causes.

Forms of hysteria such as paralyses of limbs are not uncommon in adolescence. They develop when emotion is repressed and is subsequently shunted into a limb, causing it to be paralyzed. A situation from which the adolescent sees no other means of escape may induce the same symptom.

Sam's childhood had not been a very happy one. At eight, a long and painful illness confined him to a hospital for several months, and just as he was getting well, war broke out and his father left home to join the navy. For several years Sam and his mother and his older sister were alone. He didn't mind this too much, for his father had seemed very annoyed by his illness, and his mother was very kind and patient.

The war over, Sam's father came home. He had always wanted a son who would be a great athlete; Sam's illness made him feel that Sam would never be strong. But he hadn't expected to find him so small and frail and so much more interested in music than in baseball and football. That was too much; and without saying anything to his wife or to Sam he entered the boy in a boarding school 'where they knew the importance of athletics and where they'd make a man of him.' Sam went—there was nothing else he could do—and he was utterly miserable. He had neither the strength nor the skill nor the interest to do well at games. His studies were hard and left him no time for music. People were nice enough to him, in fact went out of their way to make him happy, but he felt like a fish out of water. At Christmas he begged his father to let him stay home and got no more than being called a quitter and a sissy. His mother was sympathetic but had been told that it had been her nonsense that had spoiled the boy in the first place. There seemed to be no way out.

While Sam was packing his trunk to go back to school, the catch slipped and the lid fell on his arm. His 'ouch' brought his mother running, and though it really didn't hurt him much, he didn't seem to be able to raise his arm or move his fingers. The accident, the doctor's visit, the X-rays, the long and fruitless search for the cause of the persistent paralysis, did more than defer Sam's return to school. Out of it all his father finally came to realize what he was up against, why he felt as he did, and what Sam, with all his assets and liabilities, was like. And Sam, now out of his dilemma, gradually found his arm improving and acquired a better understanding of himself, of his father, and of why he really failed to get along at boarding school. Hysteria is hardly an ideal way to solve a difficult situation, but if its treatment leads to a better understanding of one's own and one's parents' personalities and needs, it is far from a total loss.

A young ex-Marine on his return to school also presented an interesting though less typical example of hysteria. He had been in many skirmishes in Vietnam, but he seemed unable to take even his daily tests in his stride. On going into a quiz he would have feelings almost identical with those he remembered having on the way to an encounter with the enemy. It was as though he mobilized for a little daily test all the aggressive impulses he had needed to bring himself to fight. Years of combat had accustomed him to treating every kind of emergency as a battle situation. But now in an examination, instead of a rifle with which to defend himself, he had only a pen, and in his mind it plainly did not seem mightier than his gun. Back in school, and trying to maintain his status, he found that after his long absence study now demanded every bit of concentration, so he went into an examination teeming with aggression. But in this battle zone there was no living enemy to combat, just an impassive examination sheet relentlessly shooting one question after another at him. Fortunately, in talking about his situation he could see the humor in it, and his vivid vocabulary let loose his strong feelings in a very helpful way. Before long he had seen the hopelessness in using his Marine methods in fighting examinations, and made his readjustment to civilian life.

We are all familiar with student language. Many of their words are packed with aggression, and the pugnacious attitude that some adolescents take toward studies. Such attitudes provide an outlet for their powerful aggressive impulses. Athletics are another outlet, but even with these two, under some circumstances and with some people, enough aggression may be repressed to cause a buildup of anxiety-provoking tensions.

There is still much to learn about young people; but the major factors which are unfavorable to their development of the ability to cope with stress are quite well understood. These include constant criticism and insufficient praise, excessively permissive or very rigid or inconsistent discipline or rearing practices; perennial bickering, conflict, and disagreement between parents and about their management of their children; inadequate adult models to imitate and admire; a narrow, protected environment which yields little preparation for the varied mores they encounter in midadolescence; and a failure to gain confidence or a sense of purpose. All of these obviously cry out for early prevention and correction before, not during, adolescence; later the normal processes of his emotional growth provide an adolescent with sufficient challenge. Once problems do develop, adults can do much to alleviate these difficulties. Even though the more maladjusted adolescent may have acquired only limited outlets, at least the most effective one—speech—is ready for his intensive use. By encouraging young people to express their feelings and by giving them other appropriate outlets, much can be done to prevent the development of excessive tensions.

Adolescents are in the throes of building their own personalities, of trying to become the sort of person they feel they want to be. They want at the same time to please their parents, to get their praise and approval. When, like Sam, they find that they are utterly unacceptable to one or both parents and believe that they are unsuited by temperament, interests, or skill to be what either or both parents seem to want and to admire, they have a real dilemma, and not a few develop some sort of anxiety state. By no means do all adolescents have a clear, nor the best idea of what they want to do with their lives, nor a correct assessment of their potentialities; but on the other hand some parents, like Sam's father, make decisions which are based on their own feelings rather than on their children's capabilities or personalities. Perhaps their greatest error is that they forget that adolescents are people, not puppets to be moved at will—that they are people desperately trying, at this stage of their development, to build their own personalities, live their own lives. The adult, be he parent or adviser or teacher, who stops to think and who pauses to analyze his own feelings, will try to guide and won't try to force into a mold.

When an adolescent girl or boy goes away from home for the first time to start a job, to go to a vocational school or to college, and when a younger one goes off to visit relatives or to a summer camp for the first time, homesickness may develop. Eager, apprehensive, they are tense with the excitement of a new adventure and the breaking of ties with those at home. On the one hand they are struggling for independence—cutting the apron strings; on the other, old needs stir within them and they may swing to a greater dependence than ever on their bewildered parents. All this is typical of adolescents: their desire and capacity for independence vacillate.

His new situation furnishes nourishing, though at times temporarily indigestible, food for the independence-seeking youth. Most adolescents welcome the new adventure. The real threats of strangeness are for the boy or girl who is insecure, whose early years failed to develop a sturdy personality. The ties with home, with friends, and with the familiar surroundings are being severed. Now he is suddenly unable to find his way in the dark; now his worth must be proved to strangers. For the acceptance he constantly seeks he can no longer depend on the uncritical familiarity of his old friends.

The bonds of feeling which cement a family together have various qualities. These depend for the most part on the characteristics of each parent's personality. When the father is firm and strong, but conveying deep and sensitive fondness for his children, his sons are likely to show a wish to copy his manner of doing things, and his daughters are apt to develop a love that is warm and stable. Such a man promotes solid feelings of security in his children which later allow their parting from home to be a new and exciting experience. At their going away little emotion may appear to be directed toward the folks they have left behind, but it will be a happy, confident departure filled with more feeling than they have the capacity to express.

This father may have as his wife a warm, steady, sympathetic woman, always there, always to be relied upon. She welcomed the arrival of each baby and surrounded each with the loving kindness of true motherhood while not neglecting her older children. She gave to each of her children those feelings of inner security that will permit them confidently and eagerly to venture when the powerful surges of puberty arise.

From such families come the well-adjusted boys and girls who provide us with the standard against which the occasional homesick boy or girl can be compared. Fathers and mothers like those are not as numerous in our present-day society as one would wish. Nevertheless we can be sure that there are indeed great numbers of them. We tend to become pessimistic because it is the less ideal cases which fill our newspapers and our clinics.

Homesickness, though mild and usually short-lived, derives from the manner in which the boy or girl was reared in infancy and early childhood and of the emotional climate provided for them by their mothers and fathers. Nostalgia reveals a longing for the protection and nurture that the home provides. Why does the lust for adventure and new experience so usual in the adolescent boy or girl not overcome this longing, why does it let homesickness develop? Here, perhaps, in microcosm is a transitory experience similar to mourning and melancholia.

Freud, in one of his most profound theses, postulated an arrest of emotional growth in those who, upon the death of someone dear to them, have become melancholic. For, he said, the self-blame and excess of hatred poured upon his own head by the melancholic is so counter to the natural spirit of man that some deep fault must lie in such a sufferer's development. Natural grief is a gradual healing of the many broken bonds that have been rent by the death of a loved one. The grieving person talks sorrowfully of the many merits of the departed one, and in talking begins to heal the hurt within. In contrast, the melancholic appears sorry for himself, is sunk in self-accusation, and protests guilt and unworthiness. Much of a melancholic's guilt appears to come from his vague awareness of the suppressed anger he felt for the loved one who died. Adolescents similarly have anger mixed with their love for those about them. When home is far away and this is recalled, it can produce the feelings of sadness and unworthiness (similar to the self-blame and hatred the melancholic feels) which we call homesickness. When this is the cause of homesickness, clearly its best cure is an opportunity to put those mixed feelings into words. A sympathetic ear, a listener—not an adviser, not silence, not a pep talk—will usually clear up the trouble in short order.

Camp was a grim and lonely place for Bill. This was the first time, though he was twelve, that he had left his family, home, friends, and his dog. His mother had always taken complete charge of him; she had always made all the decisions for him, so now he felt lost without her there to decide about things. Now there were no warnings or urgings especially for him; no one seemed to go out of his way to help him or to include him; the group's routine and announcements were considered enough, as indeed they should have been. Unconsciously waiting for special attention and not getting it, he felt abused and lonely. 'I guess they don't want me. I'm certainly not going to force myself on them.' Somehow he didn't like this camp or the boys there. All he did was think about home and wonder how his dog was and what his family and friends were doing. He blamed himself for not entering into the camp's activities, but in spite of this he just mooned around.

'Maybe I'm going insane. I guess I'd better write my folks and tell them to get me out of here before I go crazy. I'm sure that if I could just get back home I wouldn't go nuts.' Reassurance, attempts at friendliness, pep talks and efforts to get him into things were of no avail. Then he started writing daily cards to his parents. They kept thinking he would get over it, but when he wrote: 'Dear Mom: You'd better take me out of here before I have a serious mental disease—Love, Bill' and followed it up with 'Dear Mom—I'm afraid there is no hope for my mind unless you come and take me home; come quick, please—Bill' they thought things had gone far enough. They telephoned their family physician, who was vacationing near the camp, to look into the situation. He found Bill withdrawn and depressed, and at first could get little out of him except 'I want to go home. I'm no good anyway. I'm sure I'm going crazy.' Later he was able to get Bill to switch from talking and thinking about himself to talking about home, his dog, his parents, what was probably going on there. It took only a hint or two to get him to talk more about his mother and soon he was blurting out, 'Why did she send me away? Why won't she leave me alone?' With enough of his long-buried anger released and later a chance to put into words his stifled resentment of his mother's domination, and the chance to talk to someone about those people and things he had left behind, his mood gradually changed. He was no longer grim and without animation. A boy who had really seemed mentally ill was again reacting normally. Given other chances to talk about things at home, and without being urged to do so, he gradually entered more and more into camp life. A week later he was lively and interested in everything.

Homesickness in an adolescent is a temporary regression: it is rarely a precursor of grave illness. The girl or boy may seem quite depressed, be slow in his speech and answers, and say little except to reiterate 'I want to go home.' In short, they may give every appearance of having a serious emotional illness; but an experienced counselor usually makes a correct evaluation of the severity of the disturbance, and an understanding listener can often quickly clear up an attack of nostalgia.

In talking to a homesick boy or girl, it may be surprising how infrequently home and loved ones appear in the conversation. When this is the case, it will help subtly to switch the homesick boy or girl onto those subjects. The objective is to help these homesick youngsters express their feelings about them. You need to listen rather than talk, but your listening must be accompanied by a balanced and rounded question and comment so that you won't further increase the emotional tension of the boy or girl: you can rarely accomplish anything with adolescents by complete silence. Even in the first few minutes of talking they are apt to use old patterns of behavior and feeling that they have used with countless people older than themselves, which have developed in large part through their original relationships with their parents and older brothers and sisters. You must remember that they may respond in this way and behave toward you as they have in the past with their own fathers or mothers.

Your least expression or word will have a profound influence on this talk and on your future relationship with them. The homesick adolescent is aware only of sorrow. Good parents have always treated sorrow with kindness and sympathy so these homesick young people who are behaving at the emotional level of a hurt little child must be treated kindly, not in a severe and punitive manner. At the same time they are not little children, and although their maturity fluctuates widely, talking down to an adolescent will develop savage scorn toward his listener and he is likely to fall into stony silence.

Warm sympathy and brief leading questions have to be mixed with enough pause and silence so that the adolescent's feelings will have a chance to flow into speech. This sort of management usually produces the desired result. It relieves the young person of his guilt and sorrow and helps him to get back to normal. Unfortunately, when carried no further, the opportunity for the adolescent to gain new self-understanding is lost. However, the practical demands upon everyone's time, the lack of availability of qualified personnel, and the main business of carrying on school or camp usually make it impossible to take advantage of many opportunities such as these for getting adolescents to understand themselves better. However, when possible, the opportunity should not be thrown away.

Another method of managing homesickness, which at times works miraculously, is the simple, but not always practical expedient of temporarily sending the boy or girl home. The way that Lucy responded to this treatment is revealing. During the second week after her arrival at a large state university she had come to the college physician as forlorn an object as one could imagine. 'Doctor, I've got to go home. I'm no good and this work is way beyond me.' Nothing else would do; she just waited, adamant, for permission to go back to Mother. Daily opportunities to talk did not seem to make up for the attention and affection her parents had given her, and the weekend found her unchanged. She still sat silent and forlorn, her eyes cast down, the picture of woe. At this point her parents agreed to the suggestion that she go home for the weekend: it was hoped that this might help her out of her despondency. She left on Friday noon, and next day she telephoned from home. 'Can I come back to school? I realize what a fool I've been. I'll come back tomorrow so that I can make up the work I've lost.' When she returned, animated and eager to get to work, all her recent signs of depression and withdrawal, which had suggested the possibility of a severe mental disorder, were gone. From that time on she was happy and enjoyed her schoolwork and did excellently. To give in to a determined and impenetrable insistence on going home, particularly when no progress can be made through efforts to release pent-up feelings, is not necessarily to admit one's failure to help. It can be a very valuable therapeutic device.

A listener need not have professional training in order to help a youngster express pent-up feelings. Most of mankind has lived successfully without the help of psychiatrists, yet few have been able to do without the help a patient and understanding listener gives. We all benefit from having had a good talk with a friend, a minister, a doctor, or anyone who will lend a sympathetic ear. When we are under strong emotional pressure if we will talk, *and use words which have emotional power,* a weight of repression can be lifted and a feeling of great relief will follow.

Certain aids can be used by the inexperienced listener to tide him over those silent periods when he is likely to become uneasy and to say to himself, 'What do I do next?' Obviously it is either because of his own nervousness or conceit if he tries to solve the problem by doing all the talking. The boy or girl he is trying to help will then have little chance to put *his* or *her* feelings into words. Yet a long silence can be most nerve-wracking to the homesick adolescent. Felix Deutsch years ago devised a method of getting through these trying situations which is of a special value with adolescents. He suggested taking a significant or emotionally laden word which the boy or girl has just used and repeating it in a questioning tone. This can be done without the interviewer introducing a single thought of his own, and it breaks or prevents a threatening silence without interrupting the boy's or girl's train of thought. It is carried out in this fashion:

'Gee, I feel lousy but I don't know what's the matter with me.'

'Lousy?'

'Yes, plain lousy. I don't feel like studying, I can't concentrate. I daydream all the time.'

'You can't concentrate?'

'No, I can't keep my mind on my work; I daydream all the time.'

'Daydream?'

'All I think about is what the guys are doing back home, and what my folks are doing, and my girl.'

'Your girl?'

And so on. Such brief questions which pick up an important and probably emotion-laden word and which do not deflect or interfere with an upset boy's or girl's train of thought are very effective in getting them to express a wealth of feeling. It is a simple technique, and, of course, cannot be carried to the point that it is obvious, but if the interviewer will keep his target constantly in mind, namely, to get feeling expressed, it will be helpful. Perhaps never before has this boy or girl been able to put his feelings into words. They may have been pent up since his early childhood when he had no words with which to say them, and surely the restraints of recent years have held them back. Now in an emotional storm they clamor to be spoken against the strong repressive forces which still try to keep them buried. But in a receptive atmosphere, and with the stimulus of these emotionally laden words, the boy or girl will venture a little farther each time, gradually putting more and more feeling into words until at last they'll find themselves effortlessly saying things they had never said before.

Only with considerable training and experience can one expect to discern the emotional significance of all that will be said. Much of it may not have the overtones of feeling for the listener which they have for the speaker: rarely do even simple everyday words have equal significance for two different people. But the voicing of emotion-laden words is the important thing. It is the externalization of feeling in words and their release from the inner recesses of the mind, where they may have been causing tension, that we are after.

At times leaving home may be only the last straw that produces a girl's or boy's withdrawal from a new setting: what seems to be homesickness may turn out to be something quite different: their symptom could just as well have occurred at home.

Things didn't go well with Ann on her first day at camp. She was glum and disinterested, but she attracted no special attention. On the third day she reported to the camp nurse complaining of diarrhea. She was put to bed, and although various treatments were tried nothing helped her, so she was sent to a metropolitan hospital for diagnostic studies and advice. Exhaustive tests there failed to uncover the cause of her ailment. By this time the fact that no other girl at camp had a similar ailment and the discrepancy between Ann's healthy appearance and the persistence of her symptoms made her physician suspect that her disorder had an emotional basis. He was right.

An unhurried talk with her disclosed a disturbance which X-rays and laboratory tests could never reveal. Ever since she could remember Ann had either been ignored or treated as though she were a nuisance by her parents. She had never been allowed to interfere with their jobs or their recreation. Camp had been the last straw. She hadn't been asked if she wanted to go to camp. She hadn't had any choice as to which camp. She hadn't been told anything except that she was to go. Rejected, unhappy, insecure, and full of resentment, Ann had at last expressed her long-repressed feelings by means of this symptom, diarrhea.

Ed, too, suffered more from rejection and suppressed hate than from plain homesickness. Ever since he was eight he had been sent off to camp and school. Now, in a new school, he withdrew from his activities, ignored his studies, and paid little attention to his companions' invitations to join them. A tragic outcome was narrowly averted when he almost burned to death in bed.

It should have been obvious that he was not just homesick. In the first place he had been away from home many, many times before, and secondly he did not look wistful or depressed. What he wanted was recognition of his needs. He was determined to get attention and to get a chance to stay home *'if it kills me.'* Incredible as it may seem, his father couldn't understand why the boy should have deliberately climbed into bed and set fire to his mattress; but at least when pressed to do so, the father reluctantly consented to the boy's spending a year at home.

Homesickness will often be managed by the boy or girl himself. Only occasionally it will be as severe as Bill's or Lucy's. Rarely will it be confused with other emotional problems such as Ann's or Ed's. Commonly homesickness will be helped by such happenings as the acclaim which follows an unusually good dive, a lucky one-hand catch, a job well done, or such simple devices as being given a special responsibility or a prominent job. We have discussed the more severe type of homesickness because it clarifies by its exaggeration all homesickness, and once its real nature is known, it should be possible to handle the mild forms very efficiently. These are insecure dependent young people. They need to feel accepted, they need support from others. The role of the concerned adult is to recognize the boy's or girl's trouble and to help: that someone who has professional training and experience may subsequently have to lend his aid will in no way diminish that contribution.

7

PSYCHOSOMATIC DISORDERS

When anxiety and repressed emotions (such as hostility or fear) are expressed in symptoms (abdominal pain, difficulty in breathing, diarrhea, dysmenorrhea, and so forth) which mimic physical disease, the person is said to have a psychosomatic disorder. He may be as uncomfortable and incapacitated as someone who has a disease caused by bacteria, but he has nothing wrong with his colon or his lungs. It is his repressed feelings which are at fault and which need attention. Only when his feelings are released—only after he has been able to express them in words, not symptoms—and he no longer needs the attention his symptoms have brought him, will all be well. Obviously, first there should be an attempt to determine whether some physical ailment is responsible for the symptom, while at the same time it must be remembered that physical disorders usually have an emotional component.

Most of us feel sorry for ourselves when a bad cold or influenza confines us to bed. We enjoy, without openly admitting it, the many attentions we receive at such times. We enjoy being babied and, although we would resent being told so, our emotional state at such times is not far removed from the fussy impatience of the helpless child. This is our chance to go back emotionally to a childhood level and to enjoy behaving like someone little and helpless. All this is a common accompaniment of organic illness. Often, however, the emotions do much more than accompany, they can actually produce a physical disturbance, a symptom resembling those in a sickness. It is our emotions which produce the dry lips, the moist hands, and the sinking feeling in the pit of the stomach which is the personal experience of most of us when we stand to address an audience. All of us use such phrases as 'she gripes me' and 'I wish he'd get off my back' to express our everyday feelings.

Why one adolescent's repressed feeling will be expressed by diarrhea, another's by gasping for breath, and another's by abdominal pain or headache or a rapid heart rate is not known: perhaps in each of us one organ system is more vulnerable to emotional stress than another. In any event the emotions need to be taken into account when any symptom is present. During his late childhood and his early adolescence Ted had been exceptionally healthy and happy; he had had many friends and had done well in junior high school. He started off well at fifteen in his first year of senior high school, but before Thanksgiving he was having headaches, and he was doing poorly at school. At first his parents thought he was just temporarily having trouble in adjusting to the big high school. His teachers, who had not known him as he used to be, assured his parents that this sort of thing often happened and that undoubtedly it would straighten out. By mid-December, however, they weren't so sure, complained that he couldn't seem to concentrate, and suggested to Ted's parents that unless things changed for the better, it would be well for him to have his eyes examined: they were normal. When his marks went even lower someone suggested that perhaps it was "his sinuses" so he was sent to a specialist who found nothing wrong. Despite urging he refused to reconsider his decision not to try out for the swimming team: swimming had been his favorite sport and he had been very successful at it. He didn't go to any school parties. At mealtime Ted often seemed preoccupied, answered in monosyllables, and clearly resented any questions about how he felt or what was the matter.

When Ted's mother telephoned their family doctor he suggested an evening when he would have plenty of time and asked that Ted come in alone. 'He's old enough to go to his doctor by himself; we'll do better if you'll just leave it to him.'

At first Ted said little. He answered the doctor courteously enough, but he didn't volunteer anything: it was as though he were sizing up the situation and the doctor. He watched the doctor intently, apparently was weighing each of the doctor's few comments, and seemed to be trying to make up his mind. The tip-off came at the start of the physical examination when Ted was casually asked to 'hop on the scales and we'll get you weighed and measured.' He didn't 'hop'; his slow step, his hanging head were all the doctor needed to confirm his guess that what was bothering him was his failure to grow and to mature. It wasn't that he couldn't concentrate; it was that he couldn't stop concentrating on the things that worried him.

'Am I ever going to grow? Why am I so short? Is it because I masturbate—that's what one of the fellows said. I don't have any hair or anything—they make fun of me. I wasn't going to say anything to you. I will grow, won't I?' Getting all this off his mind helped a great deal. Once he had finally dared to come out with it, he talked freely. Then reassurance, the feeling that someone was sharing his problem, and a chance to learn about the irrelevance of masturbation to growth, and a chance to hear about and discuss thoroughly (not just once or briefly) the ways in which perfectly normal people vary from one another—all these helped. He gradually lost his headaches and his irritability and was again able to concentrate on his studies.

When an adolescent varies from his or her companions in rate of maturing, he may worry and hesitate to voice his fears, and headaches or other symptoms may develop. Few adolescents are aware that wide variation from the average is compatible with normality. To most of them, to vary from what is average is to be abnormal. We need to convince them that a variety of different states and rates of development really are normal, and to do this we must ourselves have a basic understanding of the facts of growth.

Those studies of somatic growth which have involved the observation of the same adolescents over a period of several years have permitted generalizations which are of great value. Data based on the height or weight or state of maturity of members of a given group at a single point in time are helpful, but information which is of much more valid application to an individual adolescent's growth problem is obtained from the year-after-year study of the growth patterns of the same boys and girls. From such material one learns to have great respect for individual differences in rate and time and extent of growing. Even though boys and girls are perfectly normal and free from chronic illness or nutritional disturbance, they will vary widely from one another in their growth. If adolescents have anything in common, it would appear to be that each has his own individual growth pattern—that each differs from the other.

Growth is not even and orderly. Rates of growth are best shown in charts which plot the year-by-year increments in height. Such charts clearly show that the rate of growth is not steady, that the rate of growth is by far the greatest during the early months of life, that it is slightly accelerated between the ages of six and eight, and markedly accelerated at some point between the ages of twelve and sixteen, a phenomenon which is usually referred to as the adolescent growth spurt. The adolescent growth spurt occurs in all boys and girls, but the age at which it appears, its extent, and its duration vary considerably from one individual to another. In boys it usually occurs between the ages of twelve and sixteen. It may result in an increase of from four to twelve inches in height, and produces, on the average, an increase of about four inches in height within a year. In girls the adolescent growth spurt begins earlier, commonly occurring between eleven and fourteen, and usually proceeds at a somewhat slower rate and to a lesser extent than in boys.

All parts of the body grow at this time, but all parts of the body do not grow to the same degree at the same time. Leg length increases first and is usually first to complete its spurt. The hips widen before the shoulders. The increase in trunk length and increase in chest depth comes later. The major increase in muscle and weight tends to come last. Subcutaneous fat, particularly in boys, is apt to show a considerable increase before the height spurt develops. A year or two later this fat is lost and tends to recur only when the skeletal growth spurt has subsided. In boys usually one sees a gradual increase in size of genitalia, then the appearance and development of pubic, facial, then axillary hair. In girls, one first notices a budding of the breasts, next an appearance of pubic hair, and then the menarche. The timing, their sequence, and the extent of these vary among individuals. They are important straws in the wind, however, when, for instance, a boy whose present height is at the lower limits of normal height shows evidence of growth in his leg length; or, when seeming immature, pubic hair begins to develop: these are reassuring signs and indicate that the growth phenomena of adolescence are beginning to emerge.

A measurement taken on an adolescent at a single point in time has little meaning. Two successive measurements mean more; three, a great deal. It is an adolescent's *progress* toward a desirable state—not how one finds him at a single point in time—that is important. Adolescence is not static; it is a process. That *change* is occurring in some one of these aspects of growth suggests that the usual and further changes in other respects will soon appear. It is when no change is taking place and when the skeletal age is far advanced beyond the time for such changes that one should suspect that something is wrong.

Although we constantly refer to age when discussing these matters of growth, it is important to keep in mind that chronological age can be very deceptive during the adolescent years. Skeletal or developmental age is a much more accurate yardstick to use when one is trying to judge or to describe how 'grown up' an adolescent is. These 'ages' are based on the state of the bones' development or on the state to which such secondary sexual characteristics as pubic and axillary hair have progressed. These are much more realistic indicators of a boy's or girl's actual degree of maturity than is the number of birthdays each has had. To put it briefly, when you talk about boys all of whom have a skeletal or developmental age of fifteen, you are talking about boys all of whom have advanced to just about the same point in bone development and sexual maturity. On the other hand, a group of boys whose chronological age is fifteen vary tremendously from one another in the degree to which they have developed toward physical maturity. At chronological age fifteen, boys and girls may vary all the way from less than thirteen years to more than seventeen years in skeletal or developmental age.

Normal, healthy individuals show wide differences in various growth phenomena. The vast majority of them reach a satisfactory and what may well be for each of them an ideal adult state, though their ways of reaching that goal may vary considerably. Though these are facts, and though the individual would do well, except in rare instances, to accept himself as he is and not wish to imitate some standard pattern, adults should recognize the psychological potentialities of wide differences from the usual and anticipate the anxieties which are so likely to develop in adolescents who find themselves different. Furthermore it is one thing to understand that these differences frequently occur and are within normal limits, and quite another thing to ignore them and to forget that they can be the source of real anxiety and of a variety of psychosomatic disorders. In dealing with adolescents, it is therefore necessary to appreciate how much they dislike being different and how anxious they may become when they believe they are abnormal, and to have constantly in our own minds not average data and chronological age standards but instead a clear picture of the wide variations which are still well within normal limits.

To assume that symptoms have an emotional cause, no matter how clear it is that there are emotional factors in the situation, is dangerous unless there has first been a *thorough* search for physical disorders. Signs and symptoms vary within a wide range and often demand the physician's closest scrutiny. Only a well-trained physician should attempt to distinguish between the organic and emotional elements of headaches, peptic ulcer, ulcerative colitis, migraine, asthma, backaches, enuresis, vomiting, paralysis, disturbance of vision and hearing, and other symptoms which may be due to either organic or emotional disturbance. Even when it is clear that a symptom is largely emotional in origin, that symptom or a new physical complaint may require careful evaluation and perhaps re-evaluation during the course of any treatment designed to correct the patient's upset emotions.

Judy had had a physical examination, but because she had so many behavior problems no one paid much attention to her physical well-being, and her examination had been perfunctory. She was destructive, she refused to do her schoolwork, she was insolent. Formerly she had been friendly, but now she was antagonistic. She refused to eat and had become alarmingly thin. Her parents seemed to be very gentle and affectionate and only the information that no physical ailment was present enabled them to listen to the psychologist's explanation that it was her hostile feelings toward them that were the reasons for her destroying things they had given her and for her refusing to accept their advice or their food. Logical as that explanation might have been for many such thirteen-year-old girls or boys whose behavior was similar to Judy's, her parents couldn't quite believe it, and before following out the recommendation that she be given intensive psychotherapy they decided that they wanted another and more thorough medical examination. In this instance they were wise; and no doubt any psychiatrist would have insisted on a more extensive physical survey than she had had. A fresh approach, and doubtless because now later in the illness the signs were more apparent, revealed a very different situation. The girl's very dry skin, emaciation, coarse hair, thin eyebrows, all suggested hypothyroidism and subsequent laboratory tests bore out this diagnosis. At that time she told her doctor of her former unhappiness in having been a 'fat girl,' the consequent teasing, her resentment of it, and her decision to lose weight. Wanting to eat, wanting to be friendly, she had clearly been at war with herself.

Whether Judy's hypothyroidism was coincident with, or caused by, or followed by malnutrition, one can only speculate.

We do know that she rapidly improved after she was given appropriate medical therapy; she began to eat, gained weight and strength, and again became her happy, friendly self. Medical factors or causes are not to be slighted because emotional ones are present.

Edith had always been a worrier. Despite her very high marks her hands would shake when she was given her report card and she would dread being asked to take part in a special school program that involved her speaking to an audience. At ten she had been in a serious automobile accident and after that every time she heard tires screech she would feel 'trembly all over,' and her heart would pound. Edith's mother gave her everything—all her time and attention and solicitude. She was always asking Edith if she was tired and telling her not to overdo. Her father had long been an invalid and when Edith was twelve he died.

Edith's old worries were now compounded by her mother's fears and extreme oversolicitude. Moreover, she was confused in her feelings toward growing up. At times she wanted to be like her father, a doctor; one day she had no thought except for the boy next door, the next day she 'couldn't stand him'; she dreaded her math class—'Mr. Sutton frightens me—I hate him'; and yet she refused offers to transfer to another teacher. One day she would refuse to accept her mother's suggestion that she select her own clothes and the next she would talk of nothing but her desire to escape from her mother's domination. In the midst of this vacillation between wanting to be feminine and fearing to be, and wanting to be free of her mother and lacking confidence in her ability to be, the need arose for her to make a decision about her future schooling. Should she go to college; should she go to a local college and stay with her lonely mother or should she break away and enter a school far away; should she plan for a career in medicine or just take a general course?

The result of every test in school bore on these questions, so each one found her more anxious than the last. By the time her college entrance examinations were imminent, she was so upset that her mother insisted that she must be ill.

A perfectly normal physical examination (when we discounted her excessive sweating and rapid heart rate) was in strong contrast with her long list of symptoms. 'There's a tight feeling in my chest—it's as though someone were sitting on me', she said was the most troublesome and most recent one: it certainly was the most revealing.

Many girls find adolescence no less difficult than do boys, and during this transition period old troubles may become accentuated or new ones may appear. Edith had some of the symptoms of mild heart disease and none of the physical signs. She was clearly suffering from her worries and conflicts, old and new. Some of them could be relieved quickly, but to get her straightened out and ready to live happily and efficiently took quite a bit of time. She said that talking about her feelings about leaving her mother, about her reasons for wanting to be a doctor and about her real reasons for thinking boys 'silly' and girls who pursued them 'disgusting,' helped to get 'quite a load off my chest.' At any rate, it was possible to help her through a period of uncertainty and enable her to meet daily tasks with less anxiety.

Bill consulted a physician shortly after he noticed pain over his heart, but despite the fact that his symptom was indeed suggestive of heart disease his physical examination, his electrocardiogram, and heart X-rays were all perfectly normal. So his physician told him there was little reason to believe that his pain had an organic basis. However, his pain recurred from time to time, so three months later he consulted another physician. He explained that his symptoms had begun shortly after Christmas:

he had returned home for the holidays, and on Christmas Day his father had a sudden heart attack and died the next day. Bill's examination and tests were again normal, so it seemed likely that his symptoms were a form of deep grieving tinged with guilt, and every effort was made to have him express as much feeling as he could about his dead father. Within a few days he was practically free of his symptoms. Apparently the long-forgotten feelings he had had toward his father, and the guilt such feelings had caused him, had been quickly eliminated.

Such a prompt response to treatment is uncommon but there is every reason to believe that a great deal of severe psychosomatic disease would be equally quickly ameliorated if patients could only be seen early, that is at most within two or three months of the onset of their symptoms. Early in the course of the psychosomatic illness the personality has not undergone the marked changes or built the defenses that develop when it has long persisted. Later, when the symptoms are firmly established, it is as if the entire personality had reformed around the disease process.

Dysmenorrhea, menstrual cramps, is common. But just because it is common is no reason for ignoring this symptom. The *cause* of severe, incapacitating cramps—cramps which keep a girl out of school or activities—ought to be investigated. It is not the symptom itself, but the possible causes which make us pay heed to them. Only rarely will the cause be organic, that is, due to such things as a cyst or adhesions; but a girl who has this symptom ought first to have a thorough physical examination. Often, however, our task will be to find out what this symptom is saying: in this case what is it that has her keyed up and tense, what is it that 'gripes' her. Many will need just a little attention—but that 'little attention' may be more helpful than one would suspect. Others need more help to straighten out their worries, their sources of tension. Here again we think of the things that worry girls who are growing up, who are about to become women. These aren't the matters which bother little children—or adults. It's more likely to be things like school, or death, or her sexuality: fears, wanting to be a boy, a poor relationship with her mother and a dread of growing up to be like her. These young people need a chance to get these matters straight before they develop into firmly fixed attitudes: now, not in adulthood, is the time to get at them.

When Mary was thirteen, her menstrual periods were so painful that she would go to bed with nausea and cramps for at least a day. Her medical examination revealed nothing of importance except that she gave the impression of being a very proper, very tense little girl. She was the eldest of eight children and clearly the serious, responsible one. She said she disliked boys, didn't care for parties, didn't like to get 'dressed up.'

At first Mary was reluctant to talk, but gradually, as though she had begun to realize that someone was really interested in her—not just in her symptoms—she began to lose some of her fears and talked of her many duties at home and of her resentment of her 'lucky brothers.' Once Mary had dared to say some of these things, she began to talk more freely. Other changes followed. Her cramps became less severe and her appearance less rigid and plain. She began to show an interest in her looks, had a date or two (timidly, for her mother had warned her time and time again to 'watch out for boys'), and finally came in with a new outfit, a new hair style, and the news that she had a boyfriend. The last had perhaps been a little too much for her, for her cramps, which had all but disappeared, now returned! However, the conflicts which her feelings about her boyfriend had aroused were straightened out, and we can predict that those fears, resentments, and desires which confuse and upset some girls as they grow up will no longer disturb Mary.

Though it is physicians who have the training to follow the medical aspects of disease and though they or psychiatrists are best fitted to relieve the patient's emotional tensions, it is well for everyone to have some awareness of the nature of psychosomatic illnesses. Many psychosomatic diseases, if treated early in their course, would never become the chronic cases so refractory to treatment that we now often see in hospitals. By giving early attention to illnesses and by insisting that they be seen by a physician, adults will save adolescents great suffering and permit a much higher percentage of people to be helped. To tell a boy or girl to 'take it easy' or 'forget it' when you don't know the reason for his symptoms, or when you only suspect they have an emotional basis, is far from helpful.

Whatever the emotional causes may be, the development of a bodily illness laden with emotional factors produces in reality a form of regressive behavior: a kind of behavior which resembles and re-enacts that of childhood. It is made all the more pernicious and difficult to change because it has an accompanying physical excuse which evokes sympathy and which seems to justify giving up the life struggle and again becoming a helpless child who must be cared for.

Why this kind of illness appears in some people and not in others has become clearer as we have learned more about the way it develops. Those of us who since childhood have been able to express deep feelings in words are less likely to develop a psychosomatic disease. This is a safety valve which a patient suffering from a psychosomatic illness apparently lacks, so it is in the younger years that the groundwork seems to have been laid for the future onset of this kind of illness. In adult life we may be more open in our zeal or expressions of anger at injustice, but it is the roots of these feelings which cause trouble: they go back to early life when we were unable to say what we felt.

Usually a patient who has, for example, an ulcer, speaks out certain of his feelings freely; but others, deeper buried and long pent up, he is unable to put into words. So instead of putting his emotions into words this patient 'talks' with his body. His powerful emotion is diverted from expression through the nerves, muscles, and organs of speech into those of the stomach and bowel, and there they cause pain, discomfort, and physical changes. All of us have had a similar reaction at a time when fright makes us speechless and we are temporarily unable to express our fear in words. But our vegetative nervous system expresses it for us; we tremble, our pupils dilate, and our hearts beat rapidly.

What can adults do to lessen the chance that a child or an adolescent will develop a real psychosomatic disorder? The importance of an emotionally secure upbringing cannot be stressed too much. Well-adjusted parents who have themselves under control, who have their own satisfying lives, usually produce children like themselves, tolerant, flexible, stable. A well-balanced but active home is the best insurance against future emotional troubles for the children who grow up in it. With this sort of start in life, later unavoidable experiences which might otherwise be harsh emotional shocks will be taken in stride.

Adults often thoughtlessly provide young children with a model of behavior that will later erupt into a psychosomatic illness in adolescence. A mother who invariably develops a headache, backache, or some other discomfort when an unwelcome visitor comes or when she is faced with something she doesn't want to do is setting an example for her children that may produce similar symptoms under like circumstances in them. Young children are great imitators: the behavior of elders they love may be reproduced by them, at times in a most embarrassing fashion. This is one of the ways that the seeds of a future psychosomatic illness may be sown, although adults are rarely aware that it is happening.

Adults' attitudes toward real illness—as well as their use of symptoms as an excuse—are important too. Illnesses or injuries are to be treated objectively, not feared; a sore throat or a sprain is to be treated, not just talked about and worried over.

Children who have not been made fearful and anxious by the daily uncertainties and unpredictable behavior around them rarely fear unduly such an experience as going to a hospital: adults have been kind and thoughtful to them and they have no reason to think doctors and nurses will be otherwise. To the insecure, overanxious child, they are mysterious and fearful strangers, and indeed some of them, because of quirks in their own personalities, may thoughtlessly do or say things jokingly to ease the child's own discomfort which will be taken as fact and increase their anxiety. We can easily underestimate how frightening hospitalization can be. It is not unusual to have an adolescent recall an early hospital experience in vivid detail. Fifteen years later Sam remembered his tonsillectomy at five. 'The doctor was very nice to me—he was a big man with a mustache. I remember his taking my hand when we went up a big staircase. Then he went away. Later they wheeled me down the hall. There was a tight sheet over me and I couldn't move at all. People were always coming in and looking at me and then going away as though they were looking for someone else. Then I remember someone putting something over my face. I kept trying to see it and couldn't and it sort of smothered me.' We can only speculate as to the relationship of this experience to the facial tic which annoyed him so many years afterward, but it is not difficult to believe that an experience so vividly recalled many years later is capable of causing such a symptom.

The first hospitalization is but one of many experiences that can later cause trouble. Unpleasantness in starting out at school, an unexpected vicious attack on the street, or other frightening experiences in early childhood may be more than the child is prepared to withstand.

Children can't be protected forever from frightening experiences, but they can be prepared for them. One does not hope forever to spare them, but only that they may first be made ready to meet these insults and later only gradually have to take them on. None of us really believes that throwing a child into open water is the way to teach him to swim.

8

THE SEVERE DISORDERS

As we consider the various troubles that beset adolescents, we see that they run the gamut from homesickness to schizophrenia to brain tumor. How shall such ills be distinguished, their severity evaluated, and proper treatment for each begun? Can anyone who has not had the careful training of the neurologist or psychiatrist expect to recognize these disorders? These are important questions: on occasion, life may be sacrificed because a serious disturbance seemed to the inexperienced adult to be mild.

Not even the most skilled and experienced medically trained clinician can discover every potentially malignant physical illness in its beginnings; however, he is far more likely to suspect a serious condition than any other professional person. But mothers and teachers are in the best position to discern the first slight changes in manner and behavior that warrant more careful scrutiny: they are usually the first to notice that something physical or emotional is wrong. Their observations—though their fears may not always prove to be warranted—are of great value, for many of the severe emotional disturbances of adolescence are slow to develop and are most efficiently effectively treated in their early stages. Their prompt recognition is not merely a means of quickly restoring emotional health but may be a means of averting tragedy.

Treatment of many of these ills spans a wide range. Now and then striking changes occur in the behavior of a disturbed adolescent in response to no more than a slight change in a parent's way of handling him or her. On the other hand, psychotherapy of two or three years' duration has been necessary to release some severely upset youngsters from their inner conflicts. In general, however, adolescent problems have shallow roots, and because of the flexibility and resilience of these young people they usually respond with gratifying ease and speed to proper treatment.

It should always be borne in mind that treatment of severe emotional disorders requires skill and experience. Any apparently serious problem should be referred to a trained person; even in the case of a minor ailment if a teacher, coach, camp counselor, or guidance worker finds, after a talk or two, that little or no improvement has occurred in an adolescent's complaints, a physician should be consulted. It is the function of these people to see that these young people get the help they need. It is obviously not always they themselves, however, who are best fitted to give it.

What labels should be used to designate the emotional ills of adolescence? In our opinion the fewer terms employed the better both for the patient and for the advancement of our knowledge about these problems. At present we suffer from a plethora of terms: it is as though we become uneasy if something cannot have a name or a number. Yet we know that it is a characteristic of immaturity to wish things to be clearly defined: to these people, everything must be good or bad, right or wrong. It is only with experience and maturity that we begin to see all the gradations in the world around us and can accept the disquieting variations between the extremes. Therefore, rather than to attempt with painstaking care to name most of the ills of adolescence, we believe it best for lay and professional helper alike to focus thought and attention on the troubled boy or girl. It is Ben or Alice, each with a unique background and quality of character, who is of importance, not the name of his or her ailment itself. If, after considerable thought, we label Ben 'an interesting case of psychomotor epilepsy' or Alice 'a typical case of psychogenic dysmenorrhea,' we may then focus on the illness and lose some of our interest in the person. We may then treat and think about them as we would a fixed problem, not as people whose problem only resembles those which others have experienced. Furthermore, once a label has been assigned, there is a tendency to be reluctant to admit error and to change the label and the treatment when new conditions or evidence arise which require it.

Admittedly, for purposes of study and orderly discussion, we sometimes need to use names and labels. The point is that all this is secondary, that the matter of primary importance is the individual. The adolescent is very important to himself, and he must be very important to you if you are to do your best for him. More than at any other time of life, adolescence is an age when the importance of each individual is paramount. Young people are struggling mightily for recognition from their companions and from adults around them. How often we hear them say, 'If they'd only take me seriously!' In truth this is the need of every man and woman under the sun.

It is not our purpose in the next few pages to encourage parents or teachers to become diagnosticians or psychotherapists. The intent is to give more people a better understanding of the causative factors of some of the more severe emotional diseases with the hope that a comprehension of the role which these factors play will make for a more widespread prevention of the less serious ailments. A discussion of serious disease often serves to throw into sharper focus those causative factors which also initiate minor ailments. It is important to remember that the presence of a component sometimes associated with a mental illness does not automatically mean that a serious problem is inevitable. Many adolescents survive broken homes, few boys who prefer to sit and read to engaging in sports get into trouble. Many who have been an 'only child' mature very satisfactorily. These may be warning signals—but they are just that, not a diagnosis.

Few adolescents develop real psychoses, although many go through periods when their behavior may temporarily be difficult to distinguish from such a condition as schizophrenia, one of their most serious illnesses. Indeed, at the onset and peak of much less severe disorders, when they are nothing more than temporarily confused, perfectly normal adolescents have been found by psychologists to give responses to such tests as the Rorschach very like those obtained from schizophrenic patients. Unless the psychologist is both cautious and experienced in the use of tests like the Rorschach, his interpretation of an adolescent's response will be pessimistic and, at times, in grave error. The importance of care in the interpretation of projective tests of those who have used hallucinogenic drugs should not be overlooked.

It is important to remember that after a very short time a boy or girl who has seemed very ill may swing back to normal. Though they may have been completely out of touch with reality, one cannot be sure, without several days' observation, that this was more than the response of an adolescent whose feelings have become extremely upset during a period of adjustment to one of the many stresses that upset them all. Adolescents frequently show symptoms which would be most ominous and diagnostic of severe and prolonged mental illness in an adult, but which in them are only transient and, though demanding expert attention, not a cause for despair. They are resilient, they have great capacity for change, and they are in an unsettled period with wide swings in emotional reaction. Just as with their physical growth, so must their emotional status be cautiously evaluated whenever possible, serially over a period of time rather than as of a given moment or after only a few observations.

The nature of the stresses which act as causative factors of emotional illness is not always clear. For instance, the sadness that comes with homesickness may develop into a state in which boys or girls withdraw all interest and attention from people and things about them: they may become so wrapped up in thoughts of home that their school and their companions seem unreal to them. Constantly dreaming of home and thinking of themselves, they are unable to grasp their schoolwork except in fragments, and these, being disconnected, confuse and bewilder them. This confusion worries them and they ask themselves, 'What is going on in my mind?' 'Am I going crazy?' Fed by this anxiety, their confusion soon reaches that state where nothing is clear, and they sit, the picture of bewilderment, rubbing their foreheads as if to push the clouds away, making comments or asking questions which seem to us to make little sense. This, of course, isn't schizophrenia. It is homesickness; but the day-dreaming, the confusion, the withdrawal from usual pursuits could lead one to an erroneous quick impression.

Anger, too, can be one of the bases of adolescent schizophreniclike behavior. This is not the wholesome, outspoken anger of the quick-tempered, but the smoldering, deep anger that never reaches up into consciousness. Like molten lava this kind of anger waits for the time when its pressure will be strong enough to blow off the top. As the pressure grows, it seeks other outlets and may become so great that it breeds a wish to destroy not only those for whom one has close ties but also anyone who meets one's fancy. As a protection from this wish, all people are made to seem unreal. In this unreality another disturbing occurrence may take place in the angry adolescent's psyche. Unable to vent his or her rage on its appropriate object or target, the rage may be turned upon its bearer with the result that depression develops. This depression can reach an intensity which cannot be controlled, in which case a suicide attempt or even suicide may precipitate. It is therefore of crucial importance to treat the depressed adolescent with extreme care. The less well-developed controls of behavior in adolescence may permit impulsive behavior that is as violent as it is unexpected.

Unreality is usually a fixed sensation in schizophrenia. It is as if much of the personality has been turned backward in time and functions at an infantile level: thumb-sucking, playing with bowel movements, and absorption in infantile play and mannerisms are common. All things outside are warped and distorted; all sense of time and place are lost; people seem changed and familiar faces are unrecognized; remembered voices are heard again; primitive impulses checked since early childhood tell him to hide, to kill, to attack, to flee, or even to punish himself by taking his own life. Many boys and girls have similar experiences, but of course in a very limited and diluted form. Their resiliency is great, and with the emotional support of loving parents and their own friends, they ride through such brief threats and enter adulthood with few if any scars. Again it is imperative to be slow to make a judgment or diagnosis or to predict the outcome especially when the symptoms are few or of very recent onset.

Unfortunately, however, at times these warning signals not only demand attention but prove really to have indicated serious trouble. How is it that some adolescents do not fare so well and, failing to master these outbursts, suffer temporary breakdowns, or—rarely—develop a long and severe psychosis? For the answer we must first look at the experiences of infancy. The infant suddenly finds himself in a cold, bright, noisy world where a booming voice starts his tears. As the infant grows he is subject to more and more assaults and challenges. In these years his primary need is still his mother, her love and attention and companionship. When these are lacking he becomes fearful and in his anxiety seeks the shelter and security he knew in infancy. Instead of confidently stepping out to meet the world, feeling the strength of those who support him, he turns backward, retreating within himself and toward the preoccupations and activities of his earlier life.

These fears and uncertainties are unlikely to overpower an adolescent and produce such a reaction if he or she has the security and strength that a background of loving parents brings. Hurts and reverses don't have to be avoided—they cannot be—but they will be met and overcome and the child's growth in wider activity and depth of activity will go on. New ties with an ever-widening circle of people around the child are made possible; first father, then brothers and sisters, then other relatives, then those other children and adults outside his own family whom he often sees. At the same time that the child is forming emotional ties to others, strong bonds are also being made between him and things. A floppy-eared bunny, a wooly bear take on personality and meaning. All through life, however, there is an intermittent struggle of varying intensity against deep and powerful wishes to return to the security of infancy. During adolescence these impulses gain new strength and produce unpredictable and often frightening patterns. It is then that the self-love of infancy revives: and so we see reactions varying all the way from that of the normal boy and girl spending hours before the mirror, in those self-worshipping rituals which serve as a temporary escape from the problems of their lives, to the abnormal complete withdrawal which the schizophrenic seeks as a source of inner security and reassurance.

Granted good heredity, the implications for prevention are clear. Beyond this there is little to do but to be on the alert for early symptoms of schizophrenia and at the same time to avoid the errors which are inevitable if one forgets either the resiliency of youth or the extensive turmoil and reliving of their early life which is common to all normal adolescents.

Even among normal adolescents, mood swings will be encountered. Their origins are diverse and range in intensity from the 'blues' of the average boy or girl to the psychotic and sometimes dangerous attacks of manic-depressive psychosis.

The wider swings in feeling from 'high' to 'blue' are often occasioned by the struggles of the adolescent boy or girl to reach a firm identification with his or her own sex. The incidence of mood swings in adolescents is probably higher in the male than the female because of the mother's influence during the first five years of life. At the time of the resolution of the oedipal conflict, the years from five to seven, the male child is required to give up his attachment to mother, and turn to the father as the proper model to copy. The female child has a much milder conflict. Having, as all infants do, copied mother because she loved her, she has only to resign the relatively minor attachment to father, minor because he has not been as omnipresent as mother. For the same reason it is more difficult for the male child to give up the mother and cleave to the father because nowadays the father often is such a shadowy figure.

Reaching adolescence with some of the oedipal conflict unsettled, the adolescent proceeds through periods of alternating affection for and rebellion against both parents. When, in the case of the boy, he succeeds in behaving like the father, his spirits rise and he may become mildly euphoric. When, on the other hand, he finds himself overwhelmed by his old infantile wishes to be a girl, like mother, he becomes depressed, apathetic, and dull. Such change of mood can be an indicator of how the struggle to achieve womanhood or manhood is progressing. The large number of adolescents who experience mood swings of this type points to some deficiency in our cultural habits which prevents the satisfactory solution of the oedipal conflict in the fifth to the seventh year of childhood. 'Momism' has been blamed for the difficulties of adolescent males in our society; now we may expect to find equal blame being heaped upon the 'women's movement' to explain the difficulties of our adolescent females.

The mood swings of adolescence, when met with at this level are, of course, innocuous. They may bother intimates somewhat and interfere temporarily with schoolwork and other activities, but they do not pose as serious a problem as that of the adolescent who is hypomanic. The hypomanic adolescent is, as the name implies, subject to pronounced mood swings and aberrant behavior which never reaches the level of irrationality observed in a manic-depressive psychosis.

It might be well here to explain the variations of mood encountered in all these so called 'affective' or 'emotional' or 'feeling' disorders. Some individuals have mood swings that depart from their normal moods in one direction only—down or up, depressed or euphoric. Such disturbances are called monopolar because such a person has either a succession of 'highs' or, if inclined to depression, a succession of 'lows.' On the other hand, the individual whose mood swings from a 'high' down through the zone of normal feeling to become depressed or 'low' is considered to have a 'bipolar' or 'dipolar' disturbance. Bipolar mood

disorders are more characteristic of the mood swings of adolescents and of the mood swings encountered in manic-depressive
psychosis.

To return to the hypomanic adolescent whose activities can
create considerable uneasiness among his or her associates:
when understood for what they are, allowances can be made for
them. They have unbounded energy, a flood of ideas, and an
indefatigable capacity to keep going far into the night. Some of
their ideas may be somewhat 'far out' but much worthwhile action is initiated and carried out by the hypomanics in our society. Among the more hypomanic adolescents one may meet
somewhat scatterbrained behavior—too many ideas and too little 'carry through' on any of them. Such individuals should be
considered to be suffering from a mild psychiatric disorder and
prevailed upon to seek treatment.

Extremely rare in adolescence is the manic-depressive psychosis. This periodic disease is now under much better treatment control than it was ten years ago before the advent of the
drug lithium. Interestingly enough the original discovery of the
value of treating these disorders with lithium salt was discovered
by an American psychiatrist twenty years ago. Later Danish and
Swedish psychiatrists repeated his studies and found such satisfying responses to lithium that they extended the use of it to most
of the manic-depressive patients in their care. While the physio-
logical action of lithium is not yet known, large numbers of formerly hospitalized patients are now rehabilitated and leading
productive lives while maintained on lithium.

Ambivalence—loving and hating—is one of the contradictory
facets of human nature. It seems to go on in all of us at deep
levels in our personalities with little or no surface evidence of its
activity. Why do we at times dwell on all the dire misfortunes
that might befall a loved one? One of us will fear for the safety

of a relative or friend, while another equally close in his relationship will have the attitude 'Oh, he'll be all right.' Often such fears, openly expressed, seem to be a cloak for deeper-seated wishes of quite the opposite kind, but why some of us occasionally have conscious fears for the safety of someone we love and concurrent unconsious wishes that dire events befall them is not clearly understood. Such feelings are so against all we have been taught to think and believe that they are hard to accept.

So, too, can we alternately seem to love and hate ourselves. When we are truly depressed, it is as though all our hate for another was turned upon ourselves. Feeling this way, we consider ourselves worthless, bad, and unfit to hold up our heads among our fellows. When the feeling is strong enough, this self-hatred may go so far as to suggest that killing ourselves is the only fit punishment.

The depressed or suicidal adolescent is one who has never developed beyond an emotionally infantile state, or is one who has regressed emotionally to such a level. When an adolescent does become depressed it is usually not difficult to distinguish a serious case. These boys and girls do not speak freely; their sorrowful looks, the low tone and slowness of their speech, are in sharp contrast with their former selves. Since the depression arises out of childish thinking and feeling, much of what a boy or girl in such a state says will be unrealistic. This very ridiculousness unfortunately leads adults into serious errors in judgment as to the seriousness of the adolescent's intentions. An adolescent's threat that he is going to take his life may often be a desperate attempt to gain attention, but it is nonetheless worthy of careful investigation. Even though the threat may be half-hearted, one cannot be sure; it is a chance a gambler would never take. In any event, the fact that he or she openly seeks attention so desperately, in itself demands that something be done. Too often 'I'm going to kill myself' is considered an attempt to get attention that should be ignored—'He doesn't mean it—he's just trying to get some attention, leave him alone and he'll forget it.' It is indeed an attempt to get attention, often a desperate attempt; in fact it not infrequently is a cry for help. 'What's the problem?,' not 'Forget it,' is the proper response: to do less than that is to risk a disaster.

When there is any doubt of the seriousness of a boy's or girl's intention of suicide, it is helpful to get them to talk about the means they have considered for taking their life. This may seem a foolhardy thing to do, but its value becomes apparent when we remember that up until that time this young person had kept his thoughts to himself and had not put them into words. Just putting his or her thoughts into words turns the cold light of reality on them and diminishes their power.

The force of strong feelings of aggression are often underestimated because it is not pleasant even to admit their existence, let alone their extent. Faced with a multitude of poorly disguised examples of primitive rage and hatred in our present-day society, we shun this new unpleasantness. As civilized persons we feel we should attempt to control our primal passions, and we train our children with this end in mind. Inevitably they emerge from childhood with many of their primitive impulses repressed and bottled up within their unconsciousness.

But the repression of primitive urges and passions does not seem to eliminate them. In fact, when the automatic controls aren't strong enough, they may break loose, and then the results of these breaks fill the columns of the tabloids. Or these feelings, being repressed, still continue to exert their influence and appear in many forms. Psychosomatic disorders, for instance, have a repressed rage as an accompaniment: in one, his stiff arthritic joints may reflect this person's attempt to hold them rigid so that he will not kick or hit or even kill someone close to him who has unwittingly failed to satisfy his insatiable infantile needs.

Fortunately these feelings of suppressed hate need neither break loose nor be expressed as symptoms: an adolescent can learn to relieve them in many satisfactory ways. The device of understatement is one. We say we are 'putting it mildly' in order to intensify the feeling in what would otherwise seem to be a very bland comment. Overpoliteness serves a similar purpose. And so, without words, does the too-ready smile, which reminds the skeptic of the baring of fangs! In folklore the Trojan Horse story is reminiscent of the same idea: "Timeo Danaos et dona ferentes.'

A teacher's harshness or severity, too, can really be a relief to many adolescents—though they may appear to resent it—by furnishing an adversary for unexpressed feelings. A really kind teacher, though desirable for some, may cause uneasiness in other immature adolescents, particularly those who are trying to establish their own personalities. These need someone to struggle against, so that they may test and strengthen themselves.

Ed was that sort of fellow. He had never been sure of himself. 'Ever since I was a little fellow I guess I never knew what was coming off. When I'd go home after school, I'd be likely to find my mother drunk or drinking. Then my father would come home and be angry at everyone: or he'd work late.' Later when Ed did very poorly in school his parents said it was because his teachers were too harsh and didn't give him enough attention. But Ed, like many such boys, had a very different story. The only teacher he really liked was a frustrated, sarcastic chap who really deserved the vulgar nickname by which successive generations of boys had known him. 'But you know where you stand with him. I make a crack at him once in a while and does he blow up. But I don't ever dare go into his class unprepared. I'd rather have them all that way—not like Droopy—he's the mamma's boy type. He's easy on you but I don't trust him; I turn in a lousy paper or don't do any work and all he does is ask me if I feel well or if I understood the assignment. You can't seem to make him mad.' Confused, depressed, uncertain of what he wanted or where he was going, surrounded with acquaintances but without friends, rejected by his girl ('she's the only person I ever thought gave a damn about me'), he needed strong, aggressive teachers with whom he could trade punches.

Another valuable outlet for aggressive feeling is action, even though that action is not openly aggressive in nature. Difficult problems, hard work, challenges of all kinds are desirable: they can enable boys to assert the masculinity within them and to submerge those feminine impulses they find disturbing. The increasing participation in competitive sports by girls and young women is unlikely to alter the fundamental characteristics of masculinity and femininity. If we observe the outlets for feminine aggression which have been used historically we find them to be elaborative rather than destructive. The remarkable patience that has been exhibited in the many skills possessed by women throughout the ages is a vehicle for feminine aggression expressed in an intensely controlled, elaborative way. Much as the passive and receptive ovum, penetrated and fertilized by the aggressive male sperm, elaborates the infinite complexities of a human being, so do the activities of women throughout the ages exemplify this same ineffably controlled creativity. Emphasis upon this kind of creative activity for adolescent girls will provide them with outlets for their feminine aggression as adequate as are the shock and sweat of body contact sports for the male. Competitive sports furnish a good outlet for aggression in early adolescence, though it would seem wise for adults also to encourage other and increasingly mature outlets for these aggressive impulses as boys grow up.

A job is so frequently helpful to an apparently recalcitrant boy that work itself is worth more attention than it gets in these days when education seems to many to be all-important. Education is important and desirable, but many aggressive boys find little challenge in systems geared to the average and committed to educate with little regard for their ability or behavior. Jerry refused to study, was a ringleader of a gang that stole and vandalized property. He called athletics and studies 'kid stuff.' Reluctantly, Jerry's parents—who had had little of the education they wished to give him—agreed to let him get a job. Even after all these failures they still thought it was their problem and that it was dreadful for him to leave school at sixteen. But given the problem as his, told to go ahead and get his own job and plan thereafter to support himself, Jerry changed as completely as one could ever expect. Now he had something he could put his teeth in, something mature to boast about to his friends. He earned his own money, and he was more careful with it. Later he began to see that some education would be a help.

Other more mature outlets are to be found in the competitive nature of business, in fighting for causes, and in the entire gamut of reform. At different ages there are not only varying needs for but also a varying capacity to adapt to emotionally mature goals. What is suitable for one person and what will help another are not always the same. One adolescent should give up football in college and move into the world of books; another should be thankful that colleges—or clubs—continue to offer him sports as his major outlet. Only if what is best for the individual is kept in mind can we hope to reach higher levels of emotional maturity and lessen the world's dead weight of neurotic and immature behavior.

Not all boys feel or behave in this fashion or have these needs. It is the youths who have a surplus of aggression or who become homesick, depressed, or suicidal who may need these outlets. There is no one way to treat all boys, let alone one way to handle the boys with such disorders. A fractious youngster who invariably rebels at harshness may need and be most cooperative with a kindly and gentle teacher. Only by knowing each of them and each one's needs can you hope to do what is best for him. Fortunately only a few really require special handling; most of them get along reasonably well with all kinds of people. It is when things threaten to go badly that some adjustment must be made. With those free of excessive aggression or wide swings of love and hate, in short, emotionally mature, the likelihood of depression and suicide is remote.

9

STEALING AND OTHER
ANTISOCIAL BEHAVIOR

More important than a discussion of what to do about stealing or cheating, or about delinquency, is a consideration of the reasons behind such behavior. If one is to talk about prevention, it is certainly more profitable to consider the causes than it is to consider the effect of various types of punishment. What are the characteristics of adolescents which one has to keep in mind in any effort to solve these problems?

Adolescents are great imitators. A girl who admires her mother or teacher, club leader or an older girl—a boy who admires his father, his minister, his teacher, his coach, or his scoutmaster—will imitate their gestures, walk, speech, *and honesty*. But it is difficult to develop honesty in a boy whose father boasts of his tax-evading, ticket-fixing, and shady deals, or in a girl whose mother is unreliable and is forever giving false excuses and explanations. There is little use in preaching honesty and practicing deceit. But honesty in adults whom adolescents admire is likely to be imitated.

Not only adults' conduct but also their own contemporaries' behavior strongly affect the adolescent. They do not like going against their group's mores and rules; they fear being different, being an outsider. Bad leadership in such a group can spread like wildfire and play havoc with many boys and girls. Bill, picked up by the police for stealing cigarettes, told a common story: 'I never used to steal. But when we moved I had no friends so I tried to get in with the fellows who hang around our housing project. They all steal. You can't run with them unless you do too. I didn't want to steal, but I didn't want to be left out or have them after me.'

It isn't always 'gang law.' It can be just neighborhood mores. Helen's family were generous to her, she had no excuse for stealing except her 'We all steal from that store. They cheat you. It's the only store handy to school and we all get our notebooks and things like that there. They charge us more than they ought to so we just get back at them whenever we can. They're mean, too.' Her group didn't call this dishonesty. When Helen was caught, it just made them madder than ever at the storekeeper, and they thought Helen had been stupid to be caught.

New rules imposed to correct a bad situation are rarely effective. By nature adolescents resent inroads on their independence, but rules in which they have a part, whether formulated by their family, their school, or their club, they are likely to respect. By participation in the making of rules, their independence has not suffered a setback, and they have an understanding of the reason for these rules. Such rules have two virtues: they are likely to be respected, and the making of them is a valuable experience in cooperative living.

Adolescents do not like to be pushed around. They are striving for independence, they have need of praise as well as censure, they have aggressive impulses for which acceptable

outlets must be found. They have a need for success and satisfaction of some sort. If you deny or ignore these traits and
needs, all the rules and policemen will not prevent asocial behavior. Because they are younger than adults is a poor reason
for telling them, 'Do as I say, don't mind why.' A reasonable
explanation is better, but a group conference and then a group
decision is best.

A little praise when deserved won't spoil them. Even a successful professional athlete, whom you would think satiated with
praise, notices when his home run gets little applause. Little
wonder that the adolescent growls, 'What do the bastards want?'
when his best efforts go unnoticed and his slightest error gets
carping criticism.

Equally futile are rules which deny youths opportunities to
give harmless vent to their exuberance and aggression. Athletics
are a great outlet. Kicking a soccer ball is much better than
breaking windows, and screaming at Saturday games lets off
steam. To berate them for not 'behaving maturely' is to forget
the fact that they are not mature. They will become so—and in
a healthier fashion—if this simple biological fact is not ignored.

Recognition of their needs and personalities will do more
to prevent their asocial behavior than will rules. Denial of individuality, a stern imposition of an impatient or frustrated adult's
will, can accomplish little more than to make adults unhappy
and very busy policemen. But to recognize adolescents' needs
does not mean to give them free rein and to let it go at that.
Fulfill their *needs*, not their *whims*, and take every opportunity
to teach them how rewarding cooperation can be. Taking a part
in the making of the school's or club's rules is an invaluable aid
to their understanding of the need for the rule of law.

Adolescents must learn to govern *themselves*. Home and
school and clubs which govern them, in which they have little
say in lawmaking or administration, may seem to run smoothly

but they are at best only preparing young people to be governed. There is little to be said for a method which develops submissive, dependent adults. What is needed is a preparation which gets them ready to govern themselves. Admittedly their first— and even later—efforts at self-government will be awkward and clumsy and inefficient; but they will learn, and they will respond best to those adults who continue to trust them despite their errors. The less adults show authority and impose needless rules, the better they understand young people and their needs and the more freely they allow adolescents to govern themselves and make their own rules, the better the preventive job the adult is doing. It is in this way, not by punishment and endless rules and policing, that asocial behavior is prevented and the spirit of cooperative group living in a democratic society is inculcated.

The prevention of stealing and cheating among adolescents is fundamental, but it is obviously necessary to understand these forms of asocial behavior so that they can be properly managed when they do occur.

Stealing is common among little children and it is unlikely that anyone can truly say that he has *never* stolen. Most of us can remember taking something in order to appear generous by giving it to someone we admired, or to make ourselves appear more important by having such a special possession or to replace something lost and thereby avoid punishment. These are but a few of the types of childish thefts. As they grow older, most children satisfy the needs which motivate these thefts in more socially acceptable ways, but a few never really grow up emotionally and continue to steal in adolescence. The stealing of early childhood is neither to be ignored nor punished emotionally or harshly; it is its persistence as the boy or girl grows older that demands serious attention. Even then the reason for this stealing, not the stealing itself, requires attention. Why is this boy or girl not maturing emotionally, what are the strong inner needs which are unsatisfied and are now demanding satisfaction in this abnormal way?

No infant has a sense of property rights. We expect, and are even amused, by the way a baby grabs everything within his reach, regardless of ownership. He does not feel that he should give anything in return. As he grows older, however, we properly expect him to grow out of these babyish ways and to know that taking things which do not belong to him is no longer amusing. Stealing in the adolescent is at times a persistence of this sort of infantile behavior. It will not be cured, or properly managed, unless its origin is understood and the condition which produced it is modified. A boy who was starved for affection in his early years, and who as he grows older finds little acceptance from adults or his contemporaries, may turn to taking things. These *things* may bring him the satisfactions which he has never had from *people*. In a similar way the lonesome boy away from home may take from those who ignore him to give to loved ones he has left behind.

Tom had two older brothers—when he was sixteen they had already left home—and two younger sisters. His father was rarely home: when he was home he was often tired and irritable and it seemed as if his daily work had drained his desire or capacity to understand people. Tom's mother too always seemed to be too busy or too tired to be bothered with him. Less able or energetic than either of them, Tom grew apart from them and spent most of his time with boys of his own age. He had no very close friends but he kept active and seemed happy. Then suddenly one day his father said he wanted to talk to him. 'I've arranged for you to go to your aunt's for a year: there's a great school there—they'll teach you to concentrate.'

Tom was stunned, and he protested feebly that he'd rather

stay on in his high school. He was told not to be childish, and that it was all settled anyway. So after the Christmas holidays he found himself away from home, in a new school with new companions, new teachers, and new ways. Everybody else seemed to have friends; no one seemed particularly interested in him. There wasn't much free time—he was glad of that, because he didn't know what to do with himself when there weren't classes or athletics to go to.

He'd never stolen before. But now it wasn't long before he found himself taking things. Little things, big things, things he didn't need. From anyone. Not for spite. Not to use them: he just stored them in his trunk. Finally he was caught. This time it seemed as though he might have wanted to be caught, he was so clumsy and careless about it. 'I don't know why I steal. I don't want the stuff. I just do it. I know that sounds silly. I can't seem to stop—I *think* I want to, but I'm not sure.'

This boy's stealing is clearly neurotic behavior. It will not be cured by punishment or by public disgrace. He needs friends, not ostracism; he needs a friendly atmosphere in which to develop emotionally, not the resentment and loneliness of rejection. This attempt to explain his stealing on the basis of his unfulfilled needs does not ignore or condone his stealing. On the contrary it is an effort to *cure* it by finding and eliminating its cause. Punishment, swift or deliberate, harsh or mild, never can be as effective as a successful search for, and then removal of, the underlying needs and tensions which produced the misbehavior; and then, when the cause has been found, an attempt must be made to fulfill those needs and relieve those tensions *in a socially acceptable way.* They can't just be given free rein. The boy or girl has to learn to live in a world which demands some restraint and compromise and an ability to live with regard for others. That they have stolen does not mean that they will never be able to adjust to the reasonable restrictions which civilized community living demands, but rather that temporarily their tensions were overpowering: when they are relieved a healthy and socially acceptable life can be entirely possible. Punishment alone only compounds their maladjustment and perpetuates their emotional immaturity.

It is, however, unrealistic to assume that all stealing is a manifestation of neuroticism, or evidence of hitherto unappeased normal needs for security and affection which an adolescent is trying to satisfy in this abnormal way. Stealing may at times be on no more subtle basis than that a girl or boy saw something and without further thought took it. Or it may have been deliberately planned at a time of desperate need. It is when the stealing seems stupid, when it doesn't make sense, when things not wanted or needed are stolen, or stolen and destroyed, that one should expect to find an unconscious motivation for this unsocial behavior. There may be unconscious factors in all stealing, but usually it is not difficult to distinguish senseless stealing from that which meets some tangible deprivation or which is a reflection of weak or undeveloped conscience.

Stealing of things of which an adolescent has clearly been deprived and badly wants sometimes has unconscious elements which should not be ignored. When accompanied by wanton destruction of other articles or violent aggression, unconscious factors which demand attention are undoubtedly at work. Hungry girls or boys will steal food, but if they smash furniture and stamp on the cakes they leave behind, they are satisfying much more than hunger, and much more than their hunger will have to have attention if they are truly to be rehabilitated.

There is much that is not known, there is much to learn, about stealing. But there is little excuse for swift, harsh punishment that cannot wait for thorough investigation. Adolescents learn not only from their sins and their successes, but from the way adults treat them. They can be given an object lesson in deliberation and in concern for the individual, or poor example of hasty judgment, temper, and a preoccupation with the effect of the individual's act upon the health of the group. Too often an individual's good is subjugated to that of the group: the fact that the group is made up of individuals is apparently forgotten. There should be continuing efforts to give adolescents every opportunity to observe the respect which adults in a democratic society have for each individual.

That little is known about stealing, or that swift 'justice' and thorough study of an individual case are incompatible, are poor reasons for not trying to understand each boy's problem. To study it, to deliberate, is not to condone or to ignore its seriousness. If such tactics accomplish no more than to serve as an example of rational thinking and the regard of one human being for another, much will have been accomplished.

Cheating in school is a subject of never-ending debate. Honor systems are tried and discarded and revived. Rules are made and revised and methods of supervision come and go. But cheating seems to die hard. In some schools cheating is so common that it is rarely condemned by the students themselves. In a few situations cheating is really taboo and a boy or girl who cheats is ostracized. This is the key to the situation: when *their own group* has made cheating taboo, it is rarely practiced.

Rules and supervisors and teacher-instigated honor systems usually fail. Pupil versus teacher is a traditional contest hard to forget even in these days of vastly improved teacher-pupil relationships; some teachers inadvertently perpetuate it by their 'trick questions' and 'surprise quizzes.' In these instances there is a thrill in beating the game, particularly since the opponent's position of authority compensates for his being outnumbered and gives the contestants a semblance of being evenly matched! But when a group has drawn up its own rules, and after time has imbued these rules with a mantle of tradition which commands their respect, cheating will be at a minimum.

Adolescents dislike change. They are idealists who respect and will strive to maintain a long tradition. Hence the success of the honor system at a few schools and colleges. When it is well established *and supported by the group*, no boy doubts its force or the consequences of any misstep. However, when an honor system is frequently violated, it is no better than other rules or supervision. It is then a game to beat, a game fallen into disrepute, and 'honor system' has become a misnomer. Honor systems achieve respect slowly. Too often they are the product of a teacher committee or a small group of students and the mass does not feel it has participated.

Equally inimical to the development of a respected tradition of honesty are scholastic demands which are beyond many students' capacity; assignments which are too long, grading which is too severe, laboratory exercises which few can finish— these students circumvent by copying each other's work and in other ways. Since the demands are considered by most to be unreasonable, this form of cheating is not regarded by the students as dishonest. It is the institution and its methods which need modification in such a case. Surely it is poor education to perpetuate a system which fosters cheating. A good institution will mend its ways when, after a careful study of the facts, the system proves to be at fault.

Honor systems do not depend on rule-of-thumb dismissals for every infraction. Neither a good system nor a good institution will be destroyed by tempering justice with mercy. Isolated first offenses under truly extenuating circumstances can be handled with leniency and this will strengthen rather than destroy the system. Students are good judges of each other's pressures. They have little difficulty in distinguishing an unlikely story from an overwhelming circumstance.

It is well for young people to have these experiences. They are the sort of things which prepare them for the decisions of adult life. At times they need to be reminded that the true purpose of education is to make men fit for the world, and that at times this can better be accomplished by leniency than by strict adherence to the letter of the law. It is sounder biology to teach cooperation, and the need for making more of us fit to survive, than to preach survival of the fittest.

Exceptions to rules under proper circumstances are certainly wise; but frequently exceptions or rules made for trivial reasons produce a situation which adolescents find uncomfortable and hard to understand. An adolescent wants to know where he stands. He is anxious, tense, and insecure enough anyway; and when rules always give way to exceptions, when policy vacillates between harshness and leniency, impetuosity and deliberation, and when rules are constantly changed, he becomes very confused and annoyed. When an institution—or parent—constantly changes tactics and rules, the adolescent loses respect, learns nothing about proper behavior, and builds up tension and resentment. So he says, in effect, they don't know what they're doing, I guess I'll suit myself.

Too often in such homes and schools, what adults call 'sudden outbursts' occur. They happen suddenly, but they are the product of long-mounting tension. Adults who are sympathetic to adolescents and understand them rarely incite these outbursts. They don't foster the tensions which produce them.

The parent, teacher, coach, or club leader who is interested in adolescents and their development and is not blinded by isolated misbehavior will solve most of these problems which arise. But if he or she becomes immersed in the fact of stealing or cheating, and is concerned only with *it*, there is little likelihood that either the problem or the adolescent will benefit. 'Stealing must be stamped out,' 'cheating must be stopped,' all will agree, but unfortunately those who shout these the loudest give least heed to the individuals who have offended, and talk vaguely but vociferously about the example set to others. Careful, just action in one instance will do more to defeat the problem and to instruct and mature the group than will swift punishment; and it will obviate the ill effects which rejection and ridicule produce in a young person already emotionally disturbed. Individualized treatment does not mean no punishment for anyone. It does mean that an attempt is made to find and eliminate the cause of the asocial behavior and then to treat the offender so that his or her emotional maturity and social consciousness will be developed.

Opportunities for their participation in group living and in taking group responsibilities are better preventives of asocial behavior in adolescents than are adult-made rules: early efforts to alleviate signs of frustration will do more than to devise new ways to curb them. When they do go astray, rejected, tense adolescents will almost always respond better to kindness than to power, to opportunities to channel aggression than to restriction, to chances to join rather than be excluded from a group. Very few are not worth giving the chance to discover that cooperation yields more happiness than selfishness. The adult who uses these methods for the first time will make mistakes, but as skill is gained, the satisfaction of seeing an upset adolescent develop poise and a new-found maturity as a result of such talks will far outbalance one's earlier disappointment.

How do you distinguish the normal adolescent in trouble from the true delinquent? Stealing, vandalism, and cheating all have elements of distorted conscience development. Any one of these acts may differ widely from others in degree, frequency, effect on other people, and in influence of environmental factors, but in every instance we should question the quality of the boy's or girl's conscience. What are his values? Does he know right from wrong? Is he wholly concerned with himself and has he little concern for the harm and disturbance he has caused others? It is in the area of conscience that the true delinquent differs most, but among delinquents there are many types, and a variety of degrees of severity. Fritz Redl divides delinquents into four groups: the basically healthful adolescent whose behavior is a not unexpected reaction to a bad setting; the sound adolescent whose behavior has grown out of his excessive turmoil—his adolescence is temporarily too much for him; the neurotic delinquent; and the guilt-free, remorse-free, impulsive, true delinquent who has little conscience, little personality strength. Those who fall into the fourth category are not the most difficult to understand but they are the most difficult to help. They need but cannot accept affection. They need to live in a routine, predictable, orderly way, but they can't accept regimentation. They are impulsive; they react to frustration with rage and to success with intolerable boasting.

What are the implications for the prevention of antisocial behavior? Obviously, in any individual a variety of factors may be involved. These may be chiefly related to his or her community, family, or own self—the latter being in no small part the product of heredity.

Stable, friendly communities are best. It isn't by any means just a matter of economics, of how good the housing; it's a matter of how well the community gets along; how cohesive it is; how much hostility, envy, and intergroup strife there is. If there isn't much of those, the chances are that its young people will have a feeling of belonging—and will be well-adjusted and stable, no matter how poor the housing. But if the atmosphere is rife with struggle for success or with intolerance, neither attractive suburbs nor slum areas will be free from delinquency.

People who are preoccupied with their own struggle for mastery, who openly hate their neighbors and are intolerant of those of different backgrounds, have little time for their own children; they're impatient, on the move, busy 'getting ahead.' Their children don't know where they stand. So these young people, abandoned by their parents, develop a world of their own—a world with its own language, laws, and style. They are as faithful and loyal to their own group and its mores as they are oblivious of those of adults.

But even in the most unstable, the most unfriendly communities, delinquency need not always develop and obviously only infrequently does. In such a community a good family, good relationships to his or her parents, save the day. Close ties to good people—good people at home, at school, in the church, and at the club—to imitate account in great part for the many fine young people whom we find coming out of communities which are blamed for another's downfall.

And in the best or worst of circumstances—community or family—the person himself is a factor. Of what biological stuff is this boy or girl made? Some, the fortunate ones, seem almost indestructible; others are precariously balanced. This we cannot alter, but it is important to remember. Otherwise we will frequently be surprised at how little stress one and how much adversity another can withstand.

We should remember, too, that such a thing as conscience needs to be developed. It doesn't just happen. From their early years, when still very little people, boys and girls need to learn increasingly to distinguish right from wrong. This does not mean that they should be bombarded with endless 'No's' and punished and frustrated and inhibited to the point of becoming little automatons. But controls and conscience will be needed in adolescence and they won't be there if during their early years limits weren't set and the difference between right and wrong was not taught—and taught consistently, simply, firmly, and kindly from very early childhood. It is parents who vacillate between strictness for its own sake and yielding to every whim, who disagree with one another about what is right or wrong, who write false excuses to the teacher, who play one parent against the other—'go ahead but don't let your father know'—who read their children's diaries or mail, who never offer corrections 'because the child must express himself,' who fail to foster the development of the sort of conscience and controls an adolescent will need.

For our part—all of us—we can encourage and teach the principles of good early training; combat deprivation, poverty, and want; support slum clearance and mental health agencies; encourage the development of stability and tolerance in communities; support Girls' Clubs and Boys' Clubs and other similar community ventures; give young people early and increasing opportunities to participate in their families', their schools', and their clubs' problems and government. And, since unfavorable parental attitudes and actions are frequently a major factor, an effective preventive program should include efforts to provide early marital instruction in rearing children, and mental health services to those parents who have emotional problems and difficulties in their interpersonal relationships. Before parents have children, not after, is the ideal time to prevent their children's problems. The atmosphere of the home into which the child is born—the parents' attitudes toward him and toward each other—in large degree determines the future emotional health and behavior. A cohesive household, consistent, suitable discipline by each parent, acceptance and love from the very beginning, parental good example, encouragement, and the setting of reasonable limits are the basis of emotional stability, a concern for others, and a good conscience.

If we are to lower the incidence of delinquency in our

communities, and we all say we want to, each of us must actively work for all these things. Our success will be in proportion to how good an example each and everyone of us sets, how real our interest is, how much we really want to get delinquency under control.

And when faced with delinquent behavior, we can try *ourselves* to help this boy or girl to find the cure. Sometimes we'll need professional help, sometimes a psychiatrist; but much can, at least at first, be done by those who, though lacking extensive experience or special training, have a real desire to be helpful. By all means call for skillful help when it is needed, but don't let your own low opinion of your competence provide too easy an excuse for reaching for the telephone rather than settling down to do some listening and helping yourself. Your helping hand—your genuine interest—your willingness to give of yourself and your time right at the time of a crisis, may be beyond price. Remember always that kindliness antedates psychiatry by hundreds of years.

10

ALCOHOL AND
OTHER DRUGS

During the early 1960's drug abuse by adolescents began to increase rapidly in the United States and soon reached alarming proportions. Parents, clergy, law-enforcement officers, social workers, teachers, physicians, and others involved with young people's well-being were distraught, but none were adequately prepared to deal with this devastating threat. Fortunately, its origins and management are now better understood; and, although there is still much to learn and much more to do, the drug situation is now being more effectively met. However, although there is evidence that there is now less abuse of *some* drugs in some segments of our society, there is no basis for complacency or for a slackening of efforts to curb drug abuse and to help its victims: it promises to be one of youth's major health problems for some time.

Alcohol is one drug the abuse of which continues to increase. Many adolescents, perhaps wishing to avoid the hazards of the narcotics and the hallucinogenics, or disenchanted with either marijuana or the barbiturates but seeking companionship, acceptance, relaxation, or a means of escape, have turned to alcohol. Its use—and abuse—by adolescents of all ages is now so widespread that it has become a major health problem for them. Its availability, the world-wide example set by adults who drink, ubiquitous advertising, the glamour of anything forbidden, and the prevalence of disillusionment and aimlessness are factors which have a significant effect and make the reduction of the number of those who drink excessively a difficult task.

When thinking about, or attempting to reduce alcohol abuse, a distinction should be made between the 'experimenter,' the 'social drinker,' and the regular, frequent, excessive 'compulsive drinker.' The last-mentioned know they have a problem and may accept help; the others may eventually have a problem, but will rarely seek or accept help: furthermore, if we could be sure that their drinking was only a temporary matter, would not become excessive, and that they were not among those likely to become addicted, there would be less reason to become concerned about them.

Basically, it is the reason for the drinking which is the important matter: it is those who feel they must drink, who use alcohol as a crutch or an escape who cause the most concern. Since it cannot cure a problem, tomorrow will find yesterday's problem still there, and the endless, futile, hazardous cycle will repeat itself.

Drug abuse has been defined in various ways. To many it means the consistent use of any mind-altering drug in order to gain a change in mood and feeling, *and* to continue to do this in spite of the fact that the drug can cause significant interference with natural functioning and health. Undesirable as taking drugs may be, it is obviously very different for an adolescent to 'try' marijuana or a barbiturate or gin to 'see what it is like,' or so that he will 'not be the only one at a party who didn't,' or for social relaxation, than it is for him to begin doing so because he has a problem which he feels he can neither tolerate nor conquer. In the first instance he is an experimenter; in the second he is avoiding 'being different' or seeks no more than sociability or relaxation. Admittedly the first step may lead to others and so to a habit he may find difficult to break; or he may gradually turn to 'harder' drugs and turn out to be one of those who are predisposed to addiction. Unfortunately no one can predict who is going to be a compulsive user and who will not; this is obviously a strong argument against ever drinking alcohol or taking other drugs, and a compelling reason for never urging anyone to try them—particularly as a cure for distress. It is not that all drinking and drug taking are harmful and should be taboo, it is that *most* can be harmful and that *some* are addictive, *and* that when used to escape from a problem a devastating habit may develop.

How widespread is the drinking of alcohol among adolescents? There is no doubt that it constitutes a grave and increasing problem; but although exaggerated reports may serve temporarily to arouse an apathetic sector of the public, in the long run they may do more harm than good. They may soon result in the loss of support from adults who might have been of assistance, and they tend to antagonize the young people whom we seek to inform. The fact of the matter is that valid incidence data are scanty.

If problem drinking is defined as getting 'high' or 'tight' once a week, a nation-wide survey found that the percentage of adolescent 'problem drinkers' gradually rose from less than 1 per cent among seventh grade pupils to 5 per cent among those in the twelfth grade of school. Other surveys estimate the percentage of adolescents who have a drinking problem (al-

though few themselves believe this to be the case) all the way
from 1 to 15 per cent. Clearly, there is wide variation in the incidence in different areas of this country and even in different
parts of the same city. 'Problem drinking' is definitely more
frequent in delinquents than in adolescents who are not maladjusted to society. In any event, at present it seems reasonable
tentatively to assume that among high school boys and girls in
the United States about 10 per cent drink regularly and that
about 2 per cent are excessive (problem) drinkers. At the time of
the last census (1970) there were about thirty million boys and
girls from 12 to 19 years of age in this country: 2 per cent may
seem small, but it represents 600,000 adolescents.

Those who admit to being 'regular' drinkers, often insist
that they do not drink excessive amounts: 'who wants to be sick'
is a common reply. Even as extreme shortness of breath tends to
make us stop exercising before we strain our hearts, so vomiting
usually precedes drunkenness in the inexperienced adolescent.
As they get older, however, drunkenness is more common: one
report states that 14 per cent of a large city's high-school seniors
admitted to drunkenness once a week, and 36 per cent at least
three times a year. These 'problem' drinkers are frequent, excessive drinkers, but they are not 'alcoholics.' They are not yet
consistently unable to refrain from drinking, but theirs is clearly
a repetitive use of alcohol which can cause physical, psychological, or social harm to them or to others, and which may
progress to true alcoholism.

Who are those who have more than tasted alcohol? It is
from the answers to this question that our cues for prevention
may come. First, there are the occasional, the experimenting
adolescents. Many limit their drinking to beer. *Their* drinking
needs to be understood on *that* level, not as a tragic, ominous
matter. They offer a variety of explanations: common to each is
the inference that they do not *need* to drink. Many girls, just as

their grandmothers in the twenties who tried smoking cigarettes, say that they feel they'll be labeled as 'squares' if they don't. Others think it would be exciting to try, or something to boast about. Boys may say it gains them acceptance or prevents their rejection. All this is nothing more than the adolescents' age-old search for excitement, acceptance, and self-esteem, and when it *is* all, it should not be difficult to assist most of them in helping themselves to fulfill their normal needs in a more desirable way. On the other hand, those who have personality problems, who have been rejected consistently, or who have few of those attributes and skills which make the gaining of friends and confidence a comparatively easy task, may need extensive help with their drinking *and* their personalities.

Those adolescents who are—or promise soon to be—problem drinkers tell a different tale. These aren't the beer-drinkers. They need alcohol. They say alcohol helps them to do something, to forget something, to overcome something, to escape from something. Alcohol, for them, is a magic medicine—a prop, an ally. It is a medicine for what G. K. Chesterton called wretchedness—a medicine which has no place in a sick room, no place when it is *needed*. Without it they feel they cannot cope; it allows them to relax in a situation which they have feared, to forget what they can't bear to think about, to express feelings they couldn't otherwise mention, to escape into oblivion.

All this they say, or imply. The roots of their problems go deeper, and are the same psychologic, social, and genetic factors which underlie many emotional difficulties of adolescence. Not infrequently, it is evident that they have little control over their impulses, tolerate frustration poorly, do not get along with people easily, and have little self-esteem. It is common to find that there were unusually high degrees of stress and deprivation in their early years. A higher than usual number of them have an alcoholic parent: whether this should be interpreted as evidence for a genetic factor is debatable, but it is obvious that home-life with and the emotional relationship to an alcoholic parent are both likely to be less than good. The child can never be sure of his home: he cannot trust it to be a haven in time of need or a place to bring a friend. Perpetually concerned with his or her own problems, the alcoholic parent is unable to form a meaningful relationship to his (or her) children; and the other parent, overburdened and distraught, finds little time or strength to contribute even a modicum of attention, let alone adequate loving.

Time is one of the few allies of these troubled young people, but it is a significant one. They are still resilient and malleable, and they are not yet alcoholics. Given help early, many can be salvaged. In any event they must not be neglected: their underlying problems will not fade away—they will increase, and they will become more and more difficult to correct as time goes on.

To discuss the nature of adolescents' problems with other drugs—narcotics, hallucinogens, and so on—is to repeat much that has been said about alcohol. These other drugs also have their experimenters and their compulsive users; and some of them, for example, morphine, Demerol, heroin, methadone, barbiturates, and hypnotics, result in dependency. On the other hand, with marijuana, L.S.D., and the central nervous system stimulants such as the amphetamines and cocaine, dependency is much less frequently a problem. It is the addictive propensity of heroin and morphine that makes their use so hazardous. Cocaine, though frequently regarded as a narcotic, should not be placed in that category; however, it can be addictive. Once these have been taken over even a very short period of time, a habit is likely to be formed. This habit is very difficult to break, and its victims tend to take ever larger and larger doses as their tolerance to the drug increases. Furthermore, the social conditions under which these two drugs are obtained are likely to be sordid and themselves present other dangers.

There are those who believe that the regular use of marijuana will bring little or no harm, and that its use is preferable to cigarette smoking and much less harmful than alcohol. Even if both of these beliefs turn out to be true, they hardly constitute a glowing testimonial for marijuana, and at present there appears to be a distinct possibility that marijuana produces highly undesirable long-term effects. Surely, at least until there is incontrovertible evidence to the contrary, it would be wise to consider the use of marijuana potentially harmful. Furthermore, the use, possession, and sale of marijuana are in violation of the law.

The compulsive users of these drugs present an entirely different situation. They are people who are in serious trouble, who must have expert help. They continue to take drugs, and in larger and larger amounts and more and more frequently, because they can't stop. Should their drug become inaccessible they turn to another means of relieving their overwhelming inner conflicts—to another drug, *or* by resorting to violent behavior. Their inability to control their feelings seems to be their basic problem, but be that as it may they must have help if they are to be spared increasing crises.

Surveys and clinical research indicate that most of our adult addicts began taking drugs in adolescence, and that their basic problems began even earlier. Their family situations were by and large unfavorable: parental conflict, parental inconsistency in the management of the children, preoccupation of parents with themselves and their own activities, and so on. They commonly were difficult-to-control, impulsive, asocial children from early childhood on, and when very young began trying whatever drugs they could get their hands on—glue-inhalation, barbiturates, marijuana, alcohol—and by late adolescence were taking heroin or morphine.

In retrospect it is always easy to point out that there was a crying need in early childhood to help these boys and girls—to aid them in controlling and constructively channeling their overpowering feelings. Instead they usually were punished for their fighting, truancy, stealing, vandalism, and whatever other asocial activity served as an unhappy outlet for their emotions. Later a drug relieved the pressure of those feelings and became a convenient substitute for those acts. At that point, such young people's difficulties are so complex that manipulation of their environments, opportunities to ventilate their feelings in words—not deeds, and establishing rapport with them, are no more than the first steps in the attempt to terminate drug use. In fact, these measures may precipitate violent, asocial behavior. They come best later and after there is at least some hope of an adequate substitute for drugs. All of this treatment is a difficult, lengthy task.

The prevention of drug-taking is no less difficult than its cure. Education about the properties and dangers of various drugs is worthwhile, and can be expected to deter some boys and girls from experimentation: it is inconceivable that it is not wise at least to warn them. Similarly, factual discussing of the loathesome social aspects of segments of the drug scene will furnish another warning. But educational methods cannot affect deep-rooted emotional problems.

On the other hand, mental health efforts and child-rearing instruction aimed at adults recently or about to be married, meticulous attention to the emotional health of infants, toddlers, and young children, and efforts to combat social deprivation, if thoughtfully and persistently pursued, should prove effective preventive measures.

No mention of the corrective and preventive aspects of drug abuse should omit a reminder of the need for attention to *all* members of the drug abuser's family. His problem impinges upon each member of the family, affects each in one or another way, may be strongly related to one or more, and may itself appear in any one of them. This is not to say that each and every member of the family will need help—some will not; but it should not be assumed that this or that one will not, and each should be made to feel that he can readily obtain it.

The son or daughter of the addict or abuser may fall victim to the stresses and emotional deprivation of the home; either spouse may be unable to cope with the situation; a son's brother or sister may follow the unhappy course—and for similar reasons. None is too young, too old, too strong to be untouched. So each member of the family must have consideration—not just the one who comes for—or is sent for—help. Otherwise those who might have been readily helped by early intervention and those who were striving ineffectively to cope will be neglected, and furthermore appropriate preparation will not have been made for the patient's return to a more understanding and supportive home than the one he left.

11

PITFALLS OF TESTING

A variety of tests have been designed to assist in determining young people's health, aptitudes, intelligence, basic skills, personality traits, and emotional status. Based upon careful research and long experience, many of these tests can be of great help when they are properly interpreted, seen in proper perspective, and evaluated as a part of the entire picture. Nevertheless they are *aids*. Too often tests are prematurely given undeserved weight. They can help us, but we should not rely wholly on them: we need to scrutinize and to think about their results; and to avoid an unquestioned acceptance of them as incontrovertible evidence.

A review of some of the possible factors in scholastic failure will clearly demonstrate this point. Facts concerning vision, hearing, growth, neurological and endocrine status, general health, cultural background, relationship to parents and siblings will obviously be pertinent items; and tests of intelligence, reading efficiency, skill in arithmetic and spelling, aptitudes, personality, and emotional status will be helpful. But to seize upon a single fact, such as poor vision, lack of siblings, rapid growth, low intelligence, slow reading, emotional instability, or a poor relationship with one parent as the cause of failure in school, is to court serious error. A careful search for other causes and a thorough evaluation of the meaning and relevance of the item or test, as well as a thoughtful consideration of the adolescent as a whole, are necessary. To pinpoint a fact, or to give a test and to score it, it not enough. There is a *person* involved, and thought must be given to the boy or girl and to how the fact or test result relates to him or to her. Many an adolescent who has poor vision, or who has had frequent illnesses, or who is a poor reader, or is excessively attached to his mother, or who has 'grown too fast' does well in school; too many who have good hearing, or are confident, or have high intelligence, or have grown in a more usual fashion, do poorly.

A single item or test may mean very little. How far astray one may be led by a single test is no better illustrated than by the tale, perhaps apocryphal, of the college applicant who was accepted chiefly because of his incredibly high score on a 'tweezer dexterity' test. His extraordinary degree of this aptitude had little relevance to his fitness for a college career, and this became evident when his propensity for stealing was found to exceed his interest in things academic! Not apocryphal, and really pathetic, is the story of the young boy whose annoying misbehavior in school was blamed on the fact that he was an 'only child' and therefore, by implication, 'spoiled' and 'needing discipline.' More thoughtful study revealed that his bad behavior stemmed from his worry over his failure to grow and mature as rapidly as his friends.

No single item, no single test, whether it be a simple one such as impaired vision or a more complex one such as projective test results, should be swallowed whole. Take it into consideration, but don't be taken in by it. Look at the whole picture:

don't accept a test result or a fact as the whole or the irrefutable answer. Parents are apt to choose, or to insist upon, a physical explanation for any problem, scholastic, behavioral, or emotional. Their stubborn avoidance of a psychological explanation often appears as unwarranted faith in the powers of hemoglobin, thyroid extract, and fatigue: it too often reflects wishful thinking or a fear that their past mistakes will be revealed.

In order not to overlook any matter which may contribute to an adolescent's inefficient performance in school it is well to use a check list. Many factors other than the primary cause can be important and worth correcting. Vision should be at least briefly tested. A method should be used which in addition to testing visual acuity at twenty feet, evaluates farsightedness and eye-muscle balance and gives consideration to symptoms of eye strain. To look for nearsightedness alone is not enough; farsightedness can also be disturbing. Faulty vision can and does cause eye strain, and fatigue may well be a factor in poor scholastic performance: at times it may be the only reason, but it is well to keep in mind the fact that a young person who is eager for an education will not let poor vision stand in the way.

Hearing, too, should be tested. Such simple methods as those which require only a watch, a whisper, or the gentle rubbing of the examiner's index finger and thumb can be used, and then supplemented, if there is any reason to suspect trouble, by tests with special instruments. It is well, too, to have a few sentences written from dictation. This may give an early hint of a difficulty in aural word recognition and will offer a sample of handwriting and spelling which may furnish helpful information. A handicap such as moderate deafness may not seem in itself to be a great barrier to learning, but because it makes early schooling difficult and unrewarding, it can early color the child's attitude toward school and dampen his ardor. Severe deafness, early recognized and for which allowance has been made, is less damaging than an undetected moderate deafness, which compounds itself with frustration, loss of confidence, and a compensatory apparent lack of interest.

A boy's or girl's lassitude and indifference, born of lack of interest in school, is too often thought to be evidence of anemia. Anemia is rarely present to a significant degree in a young person who is apparently in good health. A low hematocrit as the cause of scholastic failure should always be regarded with great suspicion when the adolescent looks healthy, eats well, has had no recent severe illness, and is energetic at everything but studies. However, to omit an hematocrit—as a matter of fact, to omit any part of a complete medical examination—is unwise, for when an opinion regarding the causes of failure in school is sought, a great deal is at stake. Though tests of vision and hearing or a medical examination may seem at times unrewarding and unnecessary, the occasional condition which they will reveal, and the reassurance which they offer, make them more than justified.

Thyroid deficiency is another undeservedly popular explanation of scholastic failure. When there is a true thyroid deficiency, an individual's processes are slowed down and as a result he may do poorly in school. However, this condition is uncommon. During early adolescence many children go through a period of being overweight; this is usually a perfectly normal part of their growth pattern which in time will work out in a satisfactory way. It is not wise to jump to the conclusion that the boy or girl who is overweight or indifferent or doing poorly in school needs thyroid extract. The implication that they are not normal, the support given to their development of the pill habit, and the interference with their own glands' temporarily changeable but normal way of behavior, all can do harm. If a boy is slow-acting and overweight (like his father!) for a while, or a girl's overweight is strongly reminiscent of her mother, it may disconcert the parents, but it is better to let adolescents grow and behave and develop in their own way than to attempt artificial means of modifying them. This does not mean that excessive weight is to be ignored. When there is a true glandular disorder, or obesity, or an emotional disturbance, those should of course have the proper treatment.

Rate of growth and rate of maturation have effects on schoolwork which are more difficult to interpret than the matters already discussed. 'He is growing so fast' is a common excuse, but is it a valid one? Many boys who grow rapidly do well in school; and many who grow slowly do poorly. Many who grow rapidly have more interest in athletics and mechanics than they do in history and Latin, and the probability is that their scholastic failure may be due to something more subtle than their sudden increase in height. The extra energy they expended in growing was probably adequately balanced by the increased food intake. Rapid growth should, however, be noted: in the absence of other possible causes of failure, it, or at least its concomitant emotional changes, may need consideration.

Marked variation in rate of physical maturation is a more likely cause of difficulty than most of the other physical factors because it is more deeply tinged with psychological implications. The desire to be large and masculine and the fear that he may not become so can upset a boy's behavior and performance. To remain flat-chested while her friends round out can disturb a girl who is trying hard to act in a more feminine fashion. The girl who persists in her interest in boys' games and shows no interest in dates or appearance is more upset by her failure to develop than anything except her occasional excessive irritability, would lead one to suspect. A boy who at fifteen is short and shows little evidence of advancing toward sexual maturity may become retiring, seem preoccupied, and fall off badly in his studies. Teasing in the shower-room and the handicap of his size at athletics add fuel to the flames. His failure to understand that wide variations in rate of maturing occur in perfectly normal boys makes the matter seem more serious than it need be. Retarded maturation, because of the anxiety it causes, is definitely to be kept in mind as a factor in scholastic failure.

To become sexually mature and to achieve full growth at an early age can also be a handicap, but hardly as troublesome a one as is slow development. Reliability and leadership rarely develop concomitantly with physical growth. The boy or girl who has the appearance of an adult seldom behaves like one and often suffers by failing to live up to his elders' expectations.

Matters such as not enough sleep, too many hours spent on a job or in extracurricular activities, or frequent or prolonged illness can so obviously detract from scholastic performance that it may seem gratuitous to mention them, but in these days of our absorption in esoteric explanations of human behavior, the simple and obvious are sometimes forgotten. Joe may have scored poorly on a reading test, or Ed's projective test may have shown him to be confused by sex, but that Joe is working after school and up until ten at night in his father's store and that Ed is a member of practically every club and organization in school may be much more likely explanations of their poor marks.

Easy fatiguability, too, may be a factor but it is well to remember that interest is an important determinant of the amount of energy one exhibits. A severe illness or such an ailment as mononucleosis may lower vulnerability to fatigue, but young people recover quickly, and where lassitude persists a lack of interest should be suspected. A boy or girl who seems perennially tired in school is often alert enough on the athletic field, at dramatics, or over a dance weekend: to blame late hours for their schoolroom fatigue is not only to make an error but also to miss an opportunity to help them to analyze, and themselves correct, their difficulty.

Social setting and position among their siblings are also important factors. It is reasonable to expect children born of parents of cultural interests to have a considerable interest in things academic. Parents without these advantages often wish their children to have them: some of these young people may be little interested in a way of life differing from their parents'. This is not to say that some adolescents will not show an interest in things not found in their homes, for obviously many of them do; but the interest or lack of interest which some show can be better understood if one pays attention to their family culture. It is the cultural milieu, not the extent of formal education the parents have had, that is of importance: many adults who are cultured have had little schooling and yet they furnish a better environment for the development of their children's interest in academic subjects than will some who have had the opportunity of higher education but who have passed through it untouched. Adolescents' companions, too, modify their interests. They want to be like others. When their friends have little interest in school and no respect for cultural attainments, there is less likelihood that any one of them will enter wholeheartedly into these pursuits. Efforts by adults to give more applause to those who choose to, or dare to, exert themselves in their studies will help to combat this situation. It is heartening when adults, who often modify school schedules and school attendance to fit the needs of athletic contests, also make adjustments so that cultural opportunities or academic prize-giving can supplant a classroom exercise. Adolescents seek and need praise. They are more likely to seek scholastic honors when these honors are publicly recognized and rewarded.

The 'only child' is traditionally a 'spoiled' one and by implication irresponsible and likely to do poorly in school. This is far from the case: adolescents who have many brothers and sisters also fail. It is the kind of person he or she is, and the way in which that adolescent was brought up which are the important factors. This fact is mentioned only because 'What would you expect; he's an only child' is so often heard that it has gained from repetition what it lacks in evidence. There is little reason to doubt that the boy's heredity, upbringing, emotional health, and factors in his environment are of much greater significance. The only child may have had more careful training and more opportunities, or he may have been treated in a possessive and indulgent fashion. The family constellation and setting are items to consider, but again not ones to pounce upon as the easy answer to a problem.

Medical findings and social facts do not identify all of the pitfalls to be avoided in the determination of the cause of a student's failure in school. Psychological tests, so widely used today, are also open to misinterpretation. Their results should never be accepted without careful consideration. These tests furnish evidence, not answers: they are aids, not complete solutions.

Tests designed to measure achievement levels in reading, spelling, arithmetic, vocabulary, or grammar are valuable in estimating grade placement and relative abilities. Carelessness in their administration and evaluation decreases their reliability: not infrequently there is a failure to scrutinize the tests for sources of error and for information other than the total scores. Low scores on a part or on all parts of such a test may be valid; but if there is reason to doubt them, or if a decision of considerable moment is involved, the test should be repeated. Fatigue on the day of the test, a lack of interest in the test, a deliberate or unconscious lack of effort from fear of failure or in order to 'save face,' or a simple misunderstanding of the test directions can effect the score.

Even a spelling test can lead one astray. Nowadays some spelling tests are designed as 'multiple choice.' This allows machine scoring, but it eliminates the opportunity to observe quality of handwriting and—more important—that opportunity to see how the boy or girl would go about spelling the word. A spelling test which demands only that one of three or four spellings be selected as the correct one leaves much to be desired, and may yield a deceptively high score. Whenever anyone reports a spelling rating based on an achievement test, be sure to ask if it was obtained in this multiple-choice fashion. If so, repeat it, having the words written out by the boy or girl after they have heard you use them in a sentence.

Much of the value of group tests is lost if the scores of each subtest and their relation to each other is not studied. To know that a total score on an achievement test is 105 is much less helpful than to note that the reading was twice as good as the arithmetic, or to observe that it was the poor performance on the vocabulary and reading sections which lowered the total score, or to see in the many and bizarre spelling errors the hint of a language disability. It is also helpful to know whether a low score is due to many errors or to the fact that only a small number of questions were attempted: the former indicates the rapid but inaccurate work of a poorly informed or uninterested student, and the latter of one who works slowly but accurately and who may have more potential than his score would indicate. Speed is a considerable factor in these tests, and when it is, the ability of the slow, accurate worker can be significantly underestimated.

Some of these achievement test scores may be converted into intelligence quotients and this too can cause grave misinterpretation. Under most circumstances the IQ is regarded with too much awe. When it is derived from tests whose performance depends so greatly upon schooling as do achievement tests, it should be taken with an extra grain of salt. The IQ derived from an achievement test is greatly affected by reading ability, yet a poor reader may be very intelligent. In such an instance the test score is clearly reflecting reading ability, not intelligence. It is also affected by one's performance in mathematics and by knowledge of general information so the score may depend more upon the amount of schooling or background than upon native intelligence: a highly intelligent disadvantaged boy or girl might score very poorly. It is also well to remember that these tests are at times given to groups under distracting conditions which may promote anxiety and thus affect the score.

In summary, use achievement tests but pay attention to more than the total score. Whenever there is reason to suspect the validity of a test result, do not hesitate to do so. It is better to repeat a test or to check its results against another than to put too much faith in what is, after all, an attempt to measure a very elusive and complicated attribute with a far from perfect instrument. These tests are best regarded as good screening devices. Their results are to be regarded as was the news in the *Lisbon Falls Enterprise:* 'It may be so, it may not be so, but it *could be.*'

Individually administered intelligence tests, when carefully given, provide the most valid information regarding level of intelligence; but their expense is so much greater than the group achievement tests that it is impractical to use them routinely. Up to age thirteen the Binet or the WISC is used and for older students the Wechsler-Bellevue. These tests are especially useful in the evaluation of those who have a language disability: since they do not require reading, this source of error is eliminated from the estimation of the intelligence.

However, despite their relatively greater expense and their requirement of greater skill in administration, these individual intelligence tests are far from foolproof. They measure extraordinarily well *what they are designed* to measure, but other factors than intelligence enter into scholastic performance. To say, for instance, that a boy is or is not college material on the basis of his Wechsler-Bellevue IQ can lead to serious error because it measures only one of the factors which determine scholastic success. The test does not measure drive, interest, emotional stability, aggressiveness, or passivity. We need, too, to remember that the boy's or girl's emotional state may considerably affect the intelligence rating. Furthermore, the examiner's comments which accompany the test results should always be carefully considered—not just the 'score.' A nervous, apprehensive student may do very poorly on a test; we have to be sure that we are not getting an index of anxiety rather than an estimate of intellectual capacity. These are limitations rather than faults of the test: the fault is with those who assign it powers it does not have. The intelligence test is an aid to forming opinions, but its result needs interpretation and understanding, not blind acceptance. Carl's story illustrates this point.

Enuresis (bedwetting) which had persisted up to his fifteenth year brought Carl to our attention. In his second year in high school he appeared to be a reliable, plodding, unimaginative sort and his school grades were just above passing. He resisted any suggestion that he might do better were he to drop one course and concentrate on the others, but he was clearly under continual tension lest he fail and there seemed little likelihood of conquering his enuresis while this situation persisted. When the result of his first Wechsler-Bellevue Intelligence Test was ready, it was difficult to accept its accuracy: *all* the subtest scores were low and the IQ at a level usually considered incompatible with college preparatory work. Later the test was repeated by another competent examiner and an equally low score was obtained.

Throughout his early secondary school years Carl resisted every effort to lighten his load, but eventually he acquiesced and reluctantly lengthened his college preparatory course by an extra year. He apparently had feared that to accept any help might indicate his unfitness for college work; to go through college was his all-absorbing purpose—*that* he would do, no matter what. But gradually, as he felt his determination was understood, he talked more, was less suspicious of proffered help, and lost some of his tension; but only his extraordinary drive toward his goal can explain his success. His marks were never good, but he 'passed,' he 'graduated,' and he was admitted to a college where he did well. Not to have recognized this drive, and to have accepted his low IQ as irrefutable evidence of limited ability would have been to make a tragic error.

Too frequently we meet a boy or girl who is in strong contrast to Carl. Sandra was such a one. She did fairly well in her studies with little effort. On the basis of her intelligence (her Wechsler-Bellevue IQ was 135) she was accepted by a college despite the fact that her marks were little more than passing. After two months in college she withdrew: she found it 'dull' and 'too difficult.' Next she tried an easier college which her family thought would be 'more sympathetic,' but after a few months she was dropped because of low grades. Her intelligence was just as high as her tests indicated, but those tests were of little value in predicting her success in college. Sandra's obvious passivity, aimlessness, and irresponsibility were factors which outweighed her intelligence.

Cultural background and school have to be taken into consideration in evaluating the results of even the individual type of intelligence test. The test is weighted with vocabulary and information, items which put some boys and girls of good intelligence at a considerable disadvantage. How many who glibly quote IQs are familiar with the items upon which the score is based? A look at the component parts of some of the Wechsler-

Bellevue subtests will quickly make obvious how an intelligent but poorly taught or underprivileged boy or girl might obtain a low score.

The error of trying to make distinctions or predictions based upon narrow differences in IQ is a common one, particularly in institutions which have high admission standards. The differences in IQ may actually be valid, but so many other factors enter into scholastic performance that to make a judgment upon the small differences in IQ which exists in highly selected groups is to place a poor bet. Students admitted to many colleges vary more in academic performance than they do in intelligence. This is illustrated by a recent study of a group of honor students and a like number at the bottom of their college class. These two groups had an average difference in intelligence level of only about five points. However, when the emotional health of the two groups was compared, a striking difference was found. The honor students showed a far healthier emotional adjustment than those whose academic performance was poor.

Other techniques, perhaps because they are less familiar, are often accepted unquestioningly. Projective tests have recently fallen heir to this doubtful privilege. Immensely helpful as a research tool in clinical practice for many years, they are now well enough developed and authenticated for adolescents to be of general use. The addition of techniques which reveal some of the unconscious factors in an adolescent's behavior are welcome additions to the psychometrist's armamentarium.

A projective test is a procedure which requires that the boy or girl actively and spontaneously structure and tell his response to material which is unstructured, i.e. material which does not yield a 'right' or 'wrong' answer. Such material might be similar to a modern painting or to a conventional scene depicting familiar things, or perhaps people in action. The only requirement is that he tell what he sees—what it brings to his mind. By doing this he reveals his own psychological structure by saying the sort of things he might say—or hint at—in an intimate conversation, and also those matters which he is conscious of but does not want to tell, and those of which he is not conscious— which come from his unconscious. Their value should be recognized if for no other reason than that they emphasize the importance of the emotions in scholastic achievement. Properly used and thoughtfully interpreted, they can be a great help in understanding the adolescent whose failure in school is baffling.

The Rorschach, the Thematic Apperception Test, the Draw-a-Person Test, and varieties of the Sentence Completion Test are the projective techniques most commonly employed. It may be true that these tests reveal little that lengthy psychiatric interviews would not uncover, but their ability to disclose probable sources of conflict and to set goals for psychotherapy is well recognized when the tests are administered by a psychologist with good clinical experience. One has to keep in mind, however, that most of these techniques are very time-consuming and therefore very expensive. The relatively short time required for their administration is deceptive: it may take little longer than an hour to administer a Rorschach or TAT but it will require several hours to score and interpret it.

Projective tests too have their pitfalls. A projective test may suggest that there is a severe emotional disorder, but this evidence should be supported by other signs and data. The primary difficulty may in reality be due to a lack of intelligence commensurate with the level of studies being attempted, or a preference and aptitude for things mechanical rather than academic, rather than the deep-seated conflicts the projective test reveals. It is surprising, too, how well some boys do their schoolwork while under severe emotional stress, though no doubt these boys would do even better were these conflicts removed.

Not only will a rare boy do well in spite of his emotional handicap, but also it is important to remember that a boy's emotional disturbances may not be as grave as his projective test would seem to imply. This is not a fault of the test: it may derive from a failure to remember when interpreting the test that adolescents are in a period of transition, and consequently they may give test responses which would properly cause grave concern if obtained from an adult. The adolescent who 'over-identifies' with his mother, according to a projective test today, may change considerably within a few weeks. Boys whose tests give evidence of severe emotional disturbances may be well and happy in a few months, rather than in the throes of schizophrenia. Adolescents are in a state of flux—their emotions swing wide and violently before setting into balance. This transition factor must be taken into account when projective test responses are interpreted.

Furthermore, in these days when drug abuse is all too common, it is imperative to remember that those adolescents who have used hallucinatory drugs may give very bizarre responses to projective tests. The psychologist should always be made aware of a boy's or girl's previous drug abuse experience: otherwise he will be at least confused, and may inadvertently make significant errors in his attempt to interpret the responses.

It must be kept constantly in mind that any tool is only as effective as the workman who uses it. Clinical experience, preferably comparable to the extensive amount required of the psychiatrist or clinical psychologist, is a prime desideratum in assaying the validity of psychological tests. In the hands of the amateur they, like any other instrument, may be misleading and ineffective.

It is not necessary to test and re-test and to examine and re-examine, but it is important not to jump at conclusions and to avoid stereotypes. It is imperative to devote time to studying the tests, the facts, *and the individual.* Test results are both too blindly accepted and too often deprecated; it is important to know their uses as well as their abuses, their value as well as their limitations. The audiometer, the Wechsler-Bellevue, the spelling test, and the Rorschach are all helpful instruments, but they can't do the thinking necessary if one is to reach a wise decision as to the likelihood of scholastic success or the cause of a boy's scholastic failure. When a person—and a person who is in a period of growth and transition—is involved, his whole picture, not just a few observations should be given consideration if error is to be avoided.

12

SCHOLASTIC FAILURE

Adolescents' schooling is frequently a source of considerable anxiety to them. After all, school is their business, just as is a man's job or career his business. How they succeed at it, what goes on during the school day, what it yields them in the way of mastery and defeat, acceptance and rejection, pleasure and pain—all have their impact. Facts about their reaction to school, their progress in school, and their plans for future schooling are important parts of the medical history of any adolescent. They are topics which no one who deals with the physical or emotional problems of adolescence can ignore.

Determination of the cause or causes of scholastic failure requires careful thinking. Laziness and indifference are rarely the cause of failure. Some adolescents are by nature, aptitude, or interest unsuited for some types of schooling; but many who do poorly can, once the real reason for their failure is known, do well in their former, or in a different, field of study. The first step in helping them is a painstaking search for the cause of failure: this is a process which demands careful thought and an

avoidance of hasty conclusions and popular clichés. The importance of knowing the girl or boy, as well as the test scores and a
few facts, has been discussed in the preceding chapter.

Facts and tests are necessary, and in order to avoid omitting a significant factor it is well to have a check list; but be ready
to depart from this list whenever it seems likely that information
will be gathered more satisfactorily in some other order. If a boy
or girl wants to talk, by all means let him: tomorrow he may not
feel like telling you the really important thing. You always learn
much more by listening than from the best or from the newest
'test' which you had planned to give.

Before considering in detail some of the more common
causes of scholastic failure, it may be well to make some comment about the sort of result one can expect from a study of an
adolescent who is doing poorly in school. If the result of your
effort is considered successful only in those instances where
subsequently there is a complete reversal in scholastic performance, your successes may be few. But when helping to change
a maladjusted adolescent into a well-adjusted and effective one
is considered a successful result, the percentage improved will
be much higher. The improvement of the adjustment to life
should be the aim.

Some apparently difficult educational problems arise from
the fact that a parent, or the customs of the boys' or girls' group,
has placed them in an educational setting to which they are unsuited. This does not mean that they are uneducable; it only
means that a square peg has failed to fit into a round hole. If a
transfer into another 'easier' type of education has to be made,
this may seem to some to constitute an unsuccessful result; but
impartial observers will not agree. Education is a broad term: it
covers more than one school or one course or even more than
schools themselves have to offer. What the neighborhood
school and its courses offer is the most general and convenient

means of education; that these may be unsuited to an occasional adolescent is inevitable. At times the best way to solve a boy's or girl's schooling problem is temporarily to take him out of it. A job or apprentice learning can mature some for whom formal schooling seems only to perpetuate immaturity and anxiety.

To find just the right setting or remedy for the adolescent who is failing in school is the aim of investigations such as will be described. Often neither the school, the grade, nor the subjects will need to be changed; but when a good adjustment is unlikely within them, it is sensible to admit it and to suggest a change. Change for its own sake is never justifiable—usually that is no more than evidence of exhausted patience.

Intelligence is an obvious factor to be investigated in any study of the cause of scholastic failure. Its level is of most importance when a boy or girl is attempting a course for which a superior intelligence is essential: failure in a course of study which does not demand high intelligence is most likely due to some other cause. To label a student stupid just because of failure is thoughtless. There may not be a sufficiently high level of intelligence to permit successful handling of a difficult subject, but the same student may perform well, perhaps even brilliantly, in another type of course. It is better to say that such a one does not seem suited for, or capable of, the present course rather than to call a boy or girl stupid. The word stupidity implies hopelessness. Many who have done very poorly in a college preparatory curriculum have done exceedingly well in a business course or in mechanics or art. Some who have been called stupid have later turned in excellent performances in subjects which formerly seemed beyond their grasp. Not a few of them make a better adjustment and contribution in adult life than do their more successful schoolmates.

Not only should level of intelligence be thought of in terms of the type of studies the student is attempting, but also one's opinion of the extent of its influence should be affected by the character of the student's interest and drive. As we have said, one whose intelligence is at the lower limits of that which is compatible with college work, but whose interest in going to college is great, may well do better in college than indifferent and purposeless students of high intelligence.

Inferior intelligence, however, can be the primary cause of failure. It is important to recognize this and to adjust the educational program so that self-respect and confidence can be maintained and an opportunity given for a type of training which will fit the boy or girl for a useful and satisfying life. There are courses in schools for boys and girls whose level of intelligence is too low for college preparatory work, and there are many useful skills which can be developed in the place of a smattering of French or chemistry.

Such simple matters as improper grade placement and a lack of knowledge of fundamentals should not be forgotten in a search for the cause of failure. Through illness, a family's move from one town to another, or parents' insistence that a teenager hurry through school, a student may be found to be in a grade too advanced for him. Almost always such a situation will be straightened out by the school, but it should be kept in mind. More commonly found is the effect of a poor knowledge of fundamentals. Not infrequently a pupil, through lack of interest, poor teaching, a poor relationship with a teacher in one grade, or through illness, will miss some fundamental points or training but will move ahead to a higher level where this lack is a serious handicap. Embarrassed to ask what others may think a stupid question, or perhaps inhibited from showing an interest in academic subjects by their companions' indifference to them, confused and failing, they will flounder on and seek satisfaction from extracurricular activities. These are the ones who benefit from tutoring, or, in some cases, from a change in schools.

Often 'face-saving' will block any improvement until some such step is taken. They find it difficult to ask a question about a sixth-grade matter in front of their quick-to-laugh eighth-grade companions.

At the present time one factor frequently blamed for failure in school is 'slow reading.' Out of this have grown such comments as that reading is poorly taught nowadays; that movies, radio, and television are making children illiterate; and that all this trouble could be averted if the present-day 'flash card' method of teaching reading were abandoned and the old-fashioned phonetic method reinstated. Undoubtedly there is some truth in all of this. Certainly no one method of teaching anything can be the best for everyone. But talk about the good old days should be taken with a grain of salt. Despite the alleged poor teaching, movies, radio, and television nowadays there are many children who read very well, and many who read more efficiently and more widely than their elders. The fact essential to remember is that inefficient reading can be a very real handicap and should be looked for whenever scholastic failure occurs. Boys and girls who read slowly, who plod through books and homework at a rate both painful and frustrating, soon begin to believe that they dislike reading and do as little of it as possible. By avoiding practice in reading they then become more and more inept, and fall even farther behind their classmates.

A few points should be kept in mind. In the first place all children are not able to read at the same rate. Just because a boy or girl reads more slowly than the average of the class means neither that this is the cause of failure nor that reading should be 'speeded up.' They may be reading at a rate which is proper for a person of their intelligence. Before any decision is reached, this and other factors must be taken into consideration. Nothing is gained by attempting to make a slow thinker read too rapidly. Many, to be sure, who read slowly can be taught to read more rapidly and will at the same time improve their comprehension; but when one is attempting to help a student who is failing badly, it is essential to remember that rate of reading and degree of intelligence have some relationship. Remember, too, that some people just plain do things slowly. They like it that way. Unfortunately their slow pace may annoy their parents and teachers. Nevertheless, there is nothing inherently perfect about the hell-bent-for-election pace of modern living, and it is well now and then to stop to realize that these few more deliberate people may be just as 'right' as we are. At any rate anything more than an initial attempt or two at speeding them up will probably do no more than increase their resentment, make them more stubborn, and increase their passive resistance to your more hectic way of living.

Poor reading may be a sign of a specific language disability. It may be just one bit of evidence that the pupil's failure is due to a lack of facility in handling words in any one of a number of other ways—speaking, writing, or spelling—and the failure not caused by poor reading alone. The treatment which such a boy or girl will need is very different from that which will help a student whose poor reading is caused by long absence from school, lack of interest, poor teaching, or an emotional upset; and these must not be confused with one another. Specific language disability and its management will be discussed in detail later in this chapter.

Finally, a word of caution about the inevitability of scholastic failure when there is poor reading. It is a handicap, but some will surmount it and do exceedingly well in spite of it. Like any of the other possible causes of failure, it may not be the sole or the most important factor; it causes disaster more readily in some personalities than in others. This fact also points up the desirability of looking for poor reading skill in those who do well in their studies. They, too, can be worthy of some special help and attention!

A specific language disability of sufficient degree to constitute a significant handicap is not uncommon: it occurs more frequently in boys than in girls and there is a tendency for it to appear in more than one member of a family. No one theory concerning its cause is widely accepted. On the one hand, those who believe its basis to be primarily genetic have developed a number of methods of treatment of varying degrees of effectiveness, of which that based on Orton's theory is perhaps more successfully employed than others. On the other hand increasing acceptance is being given to emotional origins of reading disability. Most language therapists stress the importance of the rapport established between patient and therapist and the value of interview techniques in facilitating emotional release.

Reading has also been found to be closely related to attitudes toward the taking in of food and toward all the bodily activities concerned with taking in and giving out. In his book *Psychoanalysis and the Education of the Child,* Pearson cites an impressive number of instances in which both scholastic failure and reading disability have been corrected as a result of intensive psychotherapy.

The boy or girl who is handicapped by a hitherto unrecognized specific language disability is typically one who was late in learning to talk, had difficulty in learning to read, is not a fluent talker, found spelling difficult and arithmetic relatively easy to learn, and has more relatives who lack facility in handling words than are found in the average family. When tested they may have very high intelligence, but will hesitate and mispronounce words as they read aloud, spell atrociously, score poorly on a reading test, and show evidence of uncertainty (evidenced by variation in the slant of letters, in pencil pressure, and in the spacing between letters, writing over, and erasures) in their handwriting. In school, their performance in mathematics and science may be excellent, but they will usually do poorly in foreign languages (though they will do much better in grammar than in vocabulary or in writing from dictation) and in courses requiring much reading and writing. Not many who have this difficulty will show all these signs or symptoms, but many will have several of them. A few will stutter or lisp, most will be unable to read aloud correctly and fluently, few will care for acting or debating, and few will have facility in remembering names or in talking extempore. Most will be very poor spellers. Not only will they fail a large proportion of the words on a spelling test, but they will make bizarre errors, reversing letters, confusing one sound for another, and omitting sounds. They will usually say that they can learn to spell a word but that this is relatively difficult for them and that they tend soon to forget it. Often, in order to avoid spelling errors, they use a limited written vocabulary, and when given their own choice of words, their difficulty may go unnoticed. For this reason the importance of giving a spelling test for which they have not studied as an initial screening device and diagnostic aid cannot be overemphasized. Some read quite well, but few as well as their intelligence would permit. Many have trouble with foreign languages because of their lack of aptitude in associating sounds and letters; unless there is some special reason for learning a foreign language, it is wise for them to concentrate upon their facility in handling their own.

The very considerable variation in degree of language disability which can exist makes it possible for it to go unnoticed for several years. A mild disability may apparently be no handicap to an intelligent child in the early years, but it will show up as a serious one when more advanced schooling puts a much greater demand upon his ability to use words. Sometimes a disability may not be noticed until the heavy reading, writing, and foreign-language demands and the higher standards of college work are encountered. This is not to say that the disability did not always exist or did not previously act as a hindrance to optimal scholastic performance. Often, however, a bright and ambitious boy or girl will not let a mild disability stand in the way of doing well in the lower grades, but will find it frustrating and next to impossible to conquer when faced with more lengthy and more exacting studies.

The fact that a specific language disability may be mild, go unnoticed, and may *apparently* be little handicap to *some* children in the early grades is no excuse for not attempting its early diagnosis and treatment. Too often, when untreated, it fosters the development of feelings of frustration and leads to a child's dislike of school and learning and to the development of behavior disorders. When proper remedial help is given these children, their behavior problems disappear in time. Once they feel that someone has recognized their trouble and is doing something to help them, they are relieved. The improvement in their handling of words comes more slowly.

The matter of intelligence is very important in this connection. Judged on the basis of school performance, a boy or girl who has a specific language disability might be thought stupid, and were this same boy to be given an achievement test heavily laden with vocabulary, reading, and sometimes spelling, he may score very poorly. Such a student should be given an intelligence test which does not depend heavily upon language ability. Not all who have a specific language disability have high intelligence, but many who do will be found to have high IQs when a Stanford-Binet or Wechsler-Bellevue Intelligence Test is administered.

A remedial method based upon the Orton theory was meticulously described by Gillingham and Stillman many years ago: it has been modified and supplemented by others in recent years. That method attempts to build and reinforce in one cerebral hemisphere the visual, auditory, and kinesthetic associations between sounds and letters. When these are subsequently heard or seen, the proper corresponding cerebral image will be more readily and correctly recalled. This method employs repeated careful drill on the sound, look, and feel first of letters and later of syllables. There is daily careful drill on phonetics and on writing from dictation, and careful training in reading with an emphasis on orderly attention to words rather than speed. When this sort of drill is given individually, attention can be given to each child's particular needs, and the likelihood of his repeatedly drilling in an erroneous fashion is obviated.

Such retraining can be tedious and dull, but in the hands of an enthusiastic, imaginative, and well-trained teacher few children fail to be considerably benefited and to be appreciative of its help. The object is to establish vivid association patterns for the sound, look, and feel of letters—and that takes time.

The importance of a sustained and repeated contact with an enthusiastic, skillful, dedicated adult whose whole attention and interest is devoted to the student during the remedial session has an emotional value of great worth. After all it cannot fail to impress most young people when an intelligent adult painstakingly devotes his or her entire attention to a matter which has frustrated and penalized them. In fact, it may very well be the devotion of the therapist and the affectionate response in the child that evokes a good part of the motivation for overcoming the language disability.

Often, too, there are new handwriting habits to establish. The boy or girl may be left-handed and may have learned to write in a clumsy upside-down fashion—though this disability is not more common among strongly left-handed than among right-handed individuals—instead of the proper left-handed position with the forearm parallel to the paper's slant. Or, being left-handed, the student may need a left-handed table-chair, or be allowed to pull up an adjacent chair, so that it will not be necessary to twist his body into an awkward position when writing. One student who came to us with the complaint of low back pain was completely relieved of it when given a chair fitted with a left-handed writing arm. When writing seated in a right-handed chair it had been necessary for him to twist his trunk into an unnatural position; and this distortion, exacerbated by the tension which always accompanied his attempts to write because of his language disability, produced major discomfort.

Illness or prolonged absence from school may be the obvious cause of scholastic failure. The frequency with which they are blamed is, however, much greater than is justified. Illness can be debilitating, but the degree to which it incapacitates and keeps a student from studying can be vastly affected by their elders' attitude toward it and by their own interest in academic life. Some, when ill, ask for their books and keep up with their classes; others, no sicker, settle back into a state of complete irresponsibility and rest their minds as well as their livers. Sickness—a bad fracture, anemia, or a low metabolic rate—may be a factor in failure, but illnesses are more often than not used as excuses which mask such causes as lack of aptitude, interest, or an emotional disorder.

A few instances will arise in which it is difficult to tell whether illness or some other physical factor is really to blame for failure. When the cause is basically physical, there will be a time relationship between the cause and the failure, an absence of other periods of failure, and an evident desire to do better on the student's part. At this point it is well to mention the importance of adolescents' having their own physician and of their going to him by themselves. Their doctor may also be the family's doctor, but it is important that they have a physician to whom they can go and to whom they can give their own explanation of their problems. This explanation may later be supplemented by a parent who feels that some point has been left out or not emphasized sufficiently, but this is very different from a parent's telling the whole story while an impatient youth sits silent. Going to their own doctor by themselves increases their sense of maturity and gives them a feeling of responsibility for their problem. In addition, it gives the doctor the advantage of hearing the story in their own words colored by their own feelings. The saving in time and error may prove considerable.

Past illnesses as well as present health can be significant factors in scholastic failure. Minimal brain damage, either overlooked or concealed by unhappy parents, may explain a gradual decline in scholastic success. When the damage to the intellect is not great, it becomes a noticeable factor only when the demands put upon it by the more difficult work of the upper grades become greater. A severe meningitis may leave damage: that it is the cause of relatively poor performance can be suspected when good school work antedated the illness.

Not all adolescents transplant easily. Wrenched from their old friends and old school by their families' move to a new town, some go through a long period of readjustment which is reflected in their poor performance in school. That the cause is really this, and not the daydreaming or sullenness which may be more obvious, will be suggested by a contrast in their previous and their present school records, and can be verified by inquiry into such matters as their acceptance by their present group. Poor adjustment to their group can also show up as a determining factor in those whose families have not moved, or in those who go off by themselves to vocational school or college. Adolescents vary in their need of acceptance by their group and in their ability to adapt to a new one, but all of them perform much better when their presence is at least noticed and when they receive occasional recognition and applause.

It is true that some boys who seem to have no friends and few companions do well in their studies. A few bury themselves in their books and excel. They too may, in some instances, be said to fail, for their way is not one which is a good preparation for effective living. Given opportunities for friendship, led into appropriate activities, they might improve their facility to establish interpersonal relationships and lead better adjusted lives.

Rebellion is often associated with scholastic failure. When an adolescent is thwarted in his effort to become independent he will fight this restraint with the few weapons he has at his disposal, even though they may not be ones he cares to use. The father who is going to make a doctor out of his son, no matter what the son wants, may find himself baffled by his intelligent son's atrocious marks; the father who denies the sense of a career in art and insists on a 'liberal education' may find himself hunting for a son who has not only failed in school but also run away from home. The harsh, critical, demanding, and never-praising father may expect to have a son who will rebel against teachers and try to annoy and defeat them at every turn. To him they are just another symbol of authority.

There is usually much more pressure on boys than on girls to do well in school, but nowadays there are social pressures on girls too for scholastic accomplishment, and these, together with parents' ambitions, make success in school more pertinent to an adolescent girl's adjustment than was formerly the case. Most of the reasons for a boy's failure in school apply equally well to them, but in addition their performance may be affected by their confusion as to their role in life and by their conflicting emotions. They need to reconcile their sexual needs and their changing attitude toward boys with present-day demands for more education and more participation in community affairs. These are new problems, toward whose solution many parents can offer little help from their own experience. Yet how adolescent girls meet them and how they readjust their childhood feelings toward boys and strive to accept the new demands of adulthood will determine their future effectiveness and happiness.

Carol's failure in school was blamed on her 'irresponsibility' and 'daydreaming.' A healthy, highly intelligent, attractive thirteen-year-old, she was as mixed up as it would seem possible to be. Not deeply unhappy, she vacillated between the most childish and the most mature comments and plans. She seemed alternately to be facing and then escaping or evading adulthood. In one breath boys were 'stuck up' and detestable; in the next she couldn't mention one's name without a deep blush. She adored her father and wanted to follow in his footsteps, but she couldn't bear to have him even touch her. She 'loathed' school, and wanted to go to a medical school. Her girl friends were 'just silly' about boys, but she didn't want to be an old maid like her aunt. 'I wish I could get way out west.'

Carol's conversation, like her mind, was full of questions: 'Why do I feel this way? Why don't I like them any more? Should I go to college? Why does my mother nag me all the time? Do you think it's silly of me to want to go to camp? Why does my father make me feel funny?'

Carol's daydreaming was hardly profitless woolgathering, and her real concern for her feelings and future far from irresponsibility. She needed time, encouragement, and an opportunity to discuss her feelings and questions—she needed insight, not nagging, not impatience.

Girls strive to be like their friends. This makes them fearful to be alone or to be different. At the same time a girl wants to be herself, to maintain her individuality. Some meet this problem by adopting an outer conformity; others ignore it, evade it, or postpone efforts to solve it. They may be mature and very realistic in one area and evasive and childish in another, accepting responsibility at school and in clubs, but remaining dependent at home.

A boy's relationship to and attitude toward adult males is a potent factor in his scholastic success. If his feeling toward his father is one of aggression and antagonism, if he no longer has any desire to please or emulate him, he may make little effort in his studies. When his relationship to his father is a good one, however, his attitude toward his teachers and his school is likely to be good. Usually a boy's antagonism toward his father will not be obvious. The boy may often not be aware of it himself, and over a period of years he may have come to accept their relationship as the usual state of affairs rather than as undesirable and unusual. Not having anyone to whom he can express these feelings, suppressing them and never facing them himself, they exert an even more powerful influence on his behavior.

Ed's parents were generally regarded as fine citizens. Intelligent, able college graduates, they took an active part in many of their community's affairs. His father ran a large industrial plant very successfully, was frequently off on trips, usually worked late, and came home tired and was 'not to be disturbed': his weekends were devoted to travel or to golf, which 'kept up his business contacts.' When Ed was fourteen his father decided to send him to what he thought was a fine school 'which would teach him how to study.' It didn't, and Ed got into just as much trouble as he dared. The letters home about his misconduct infuriated his father, and did not disturb—in fact seemed to please—Ed. In his final year, now seventeen, he dared more and more, and was finally asked to leave.

Ed freely admitted that he had deliberately provoked having himself expelled. 'I told my father the school was no good and that I didn't want to stay there, but he's always right, he always has to have his own way, and anyway he's too busy to listen. This was the only way I could beat him. I have no respect for the school. They make rules but they don't dare enforce them. They finally had to!'

Drinking, out all night, breaking rules, he was rebelling against his father's domination and showing his disregard of a father and a school he didn't respect. The teachers were as much fair game as his father. Never close to his father, never wanting to be like him, and having found no man at this school whom he would like to imitate, he floundered hopelessly when faced with the need to grow up and to become an effective man. Confused and dependent, he needed strong but warm and understanding support.

A busy father, whether affluent or poor, struggling or successful, needs to give thought to the importance of finding time to interest himself in his son and to be generous in praising early efforts. Too often in an effort to cancel what seems to him a mother's too-easy praise, he makes himself appear heartless and without affection. What he would protest is only for the boy's own good may in reality widen the gulf between them. From that point on, it is less likely that the boy will ask his opinion or seek his praise; instead he may become increasingly attached to his mother, hardly a desirable state in his adolescent years.

Not infrequently a poor father-son relationship will apparently act as a strong motivating force; but it is important to realize that such a one is neither healthy nor efficient. The boy who does well to spite his father would undoubtedly do still better were he free of this feeling. He certainly would be a much more emotionally healthy individual without it. The embittered boy who, when asked what he is going to do after graduation blurts out that the first thing he is going to do is to stuff his diploma down his father's throat, may have studied hard to win that diploma but may be less well off than a boy who hasn't one; it is better to have good feelings toward one's father (or to have learned how to cope with adverse feelings) than to have a diploma won only to spite him.

No better, either for the boy or for his studies, than a poor relationship with his father is an adolescent's too-close attachment to his mother. These are the passive, dependent, spiritless boys with little drive or purpose of their own. Pleasant but ineffective, they fail to utilize their capacities and profess no understanding of why they should do so. Dependent, they fear the failure that might come if they were to try their own wings. Lacking all semblance of aggression, they avoid the responsibilities and efforts which success would subsequently demand of them. Afraid to take on the demands of a man's role, they make a virtue of their apathy and deprecate others' show of reasonable ambition.

Anger over real or fancied unfairness or even cruelty does not always come out in word or action but may be suppressed; then, because of its power and need to be discharged, it will seek devious outlets, which may seem to have no connection with their true source.

Steve felt he had better leave school and go to work. As a freshman and sophomore he had made consistently high grades in all his subjects and he had taken part in many extracurricular activities and had held a part time job. He told of the struggles his parents had had in their early years. His mother possessed boundless energy: a powerful woman who ruled the entire family with a smothering authority. Despite the fact that he was now twenty years of age, he had only recently been allowed to drive the family car at all, and never when his mother went along; she invariably took the wheel and drove, with little regard for others.

Steve told of an episode in which he had decided to buy some clothes. After mentioning his intention at supper, no more was said, but early the following morning his mother went into town and bought him what she thought he needed. Though he now related this episode angrily, when it had occurred he had maintained his usual silence, so he was encouraged to talk about it and to recall and talk about similar episodes. Gradually more and more of his anger and resentment toward his mother came out, and as they did his attitude toward school changed. He began to see school as a means of avoiding the domination of his mother and as a means of preparing himself for the showdown with her. At the Christmas vacation period there was a violent scene, but when his new-found independence became evident, his mother saw the great need her son had to assert himself and began to yield, and slowly the entire atmosphere of the home took on a different character.

For many years this boy had rebelled against his mother's rule silently and subtly with great hostility, but most ineffectively and disastrously, not being at all aware of the way in which his rebellion was influencing his behavior. He had fought the dependency his mother imposed on him by every means at his disposal but the right one, namely, talking it out and getting to understand what caused his discontent and failure.

Every adult has within himself infantile and childish and adolescent ways of responding to life that he has never given up or left behind in their proper places in his life. These old unresolved habits of feeling and acting cause various types of emotional illness. Ron, though a college senior, was typical of many who are in their teens. After three very good years at the state university, where his athletic ability had almost fully supported him, he was now failing in his work, unable to concentrate, wanted to leave school, and was completely discouraged. He had lived alone with his mother since the age of two, when his father had left. Lacking a male to imitate and a father to help him in the normal breaking of his dependent and affectionate ties with his mother, he had continued to behave emotionally like a child of five or six. His ties to his mother were still intense at eighteen.

In contrast to his violent feeling of attachment to his mother, his attitude toward girls of his own age was marked by shyness, discomfiture in their company, and a constant state of reverie about making love to them. Dreaming of being their hero had taken much time that Ron should have used for study. His fixation at a childhood level of feeling was so strong that it seemed as though he had transferred much of this emotion to his alma mater. As a result he had a deep-seated dread of graduating from college and of going out into the competitive world of adult life. It soon became clear that to ward off this threat he had unconsciously tried to fail so that he could return to college for another year.

Depending upon a college as a mother substitute is not uncommon. Numbers of brilliant but emotionally immature, dependent people unconsciously avoid the aggressive and competitive world of adulthood by pursuing year after year an interminable program of advanced study. In their late twenties, still hangers-on at a university, they have little academic standing but are content to eke out a very modest livelihood in order that they may remain within the protection of its walls.

A close attachment to his mother is proper and healthy in a boy's early years and should continue as an affectionate relationship as he grows older; but as a boy develops he should become increasingly independent and show a more and more positive relationship toward adult males and their roles. He needs more confidence in himself and less support as he grows older, more opportunities to do things and to make decisions himself. Boys need not become aggressively selfish, but they need to be allowed to develop their own initiative and a chance to imitate effective males rather than to bask in the shelter and support of their own mothers, or later with such substitutes as alma mater.

Adolescent boys vary in native degree of maleness or masculinity, independence and aggressiveness, as in other characteristics. Some break from their mothers early and assume masculine roles and relationships when barely entering their teens. Others, despite their mothers' determined efforts to cut the apron strings, are slow to show initiative and to take on responsibility. There is no set age or state of development which is normal or average for this change from dependence to independence, from mother attachment to a positive relationship with adult males. There is only the need that this transition be recognized and abetted, not thwarted. It can be disastrous to throw a boy overboard and tell him to sink or swim, but it is equally unwise not to give him every chance to learn to strike out for himself. Some will need more help and patience than others; some will not be ready to try at as early an age as others; but all should be given the opportunity. Too much protection, too long continued, destroys their initiative and is poor preparation for their adult life.

Finally, remember that an inept student today, instead of being stupid and hopeless, may in reality be a 'slow starter.' Many a mediocre student has blossomed out into a real scholar in later years: patience with them and confidence in them can be more rewarding than a too-hasty and too-strong adverse opinion. Unfortunately the converse is also true: some who blossom so brightly and so young, fade quickly.

To sum up, the causes of scholastic failure are many, but not beyond the understanding of any who will take the trouble to make a careful and patient study of the boy or girl in trouble. Laziness, stupidity, and lack of power to concentrate are overworked and facile explanations that usually indicate meager understanding on their user's part. The factors briefly outlined and illustrated here are more likely causes. At times no definite cause can be found but sometimes though none is found, the student will begin to improve.

13

WHAT PRICE SUCCESS?

Αll of us who are deeply concerned with young people's futures, behavior, and emotional health cannot be other than disturbed by the avid pursuit in our time of knowledge for the sake of the power and the material success it can yield. A society with such a goal tends to give little attention to the fostering of those *beliefs* that ensure that *knowledge* will be used with prudence and compassion, and furthermore tends to belittle its citizens of good character who do not possess academic skill. To depreciate those people and the skills and careers that are theirs, and to give no more than secondary consideration to the set of values men live by, is inevitably to contribute to the world's troubles. Even as we wish to enlarge our knowledge, we need also to cultivate the power to use it altruistically; and while we wish to encourage and praise those who are capable of learning and achievement, we also need to avoid generating feelings of worthlessness in others.

'I don't care what anyone says. I know what makes sense. If he's going to get ahead, if he's going to amount to anything, if he's going to get a good job, he's got to go to college. And it can't be any old college. I want Billy to go to a good college—one that I can be proud of. So starting right now, no matter what you say, he's going to cut out this talk about leaving school, he's going to give up his dramatics and that girl, and he isn't going to spend all that time reading. Poetry never got anybody anywhere. Mathematics and science are what you need nowadays; I'm glad he's finished with History. I'm going to see to it that he gets good marks; I want him to get ahead.'

This sort of thinking is commonplace: when it is countered with the objection that our major concern should be the development of a *good* citizen, not merely a successful one, the most restrained reply that can be hoped for is that it would indeed be nice if we lived in such a world.

Other adults, whose horizons are less limited, deplore what they refer to as the grim realities of our present-day education-career situation. They deplore today's relegation of ethical values to second place and the breathless competition for 'marks.' They are concerned about the fate of those who do not excel. What, they ask, is there for them: success may not be everything, but what will keep apathy and despair from those who do not gain it? To these adults, success would appear to be essential to continued effort, to hope, to happiness. They seemingly believe that without it, a young person has no other source of satisfaction, will feel worthless, and will wither on the vine. However, to regard education *primarily* as a means of getting ahead and a good job as its goal, or to feel that despair is the inevitable lot of those who do not rise to the top, is to place material success on a pedestal it does not deserve, and to ignore the mainsprings of man's real success and happiness. Virtues such as compassion, caring for others, honest effort, are open to all: for those who seek them there can hardly be real failure, or valid reason for despair.

The first of two related problems that very seriously concern many adults today is the relatively scant attention now given to the development of conscience and a set of values. These have given way to those pursuits likely to yield material success. The awards for excellence in studies are many; virtue, perhaps properly, is left to be strictly its own reward.

Given a directive, challenged to develop the intellect to its fullest, the busy schools have in large part left the task of developing an adolescent's conscience and increasing his awareness of his responsibilities to the family and to the church. Highly commendable as it is to uphold standards of academic excellence, to stimulate young people to use their latent talents, to refuse to accept indifferent performance or perpetuate mediocrity, yet it is clearly shortsighted to strive to give young people the power of knowledge without just as actively helping them gain a conscience concerned with the common good. This does not require additional budget, time, or staff. Our new knowledge, and the new and greater power of those who possess it, gives little ground for complacency: the age-old problems are still with us. We need more than men who can harness the atom, compute in thousandths of a second, or travel faster than sound. The primary goal of man caring for his fellow man has not yet been achieved.

The second problem concerns the effects which the premium placed upon academic success has had upon those young people who are unable to do well in school. Anyone who has a concern for young people's emotional health, happiness, and productivity must be disturbed by the damage which constant, albeit inadvertent, belittling does to those who do not do well, or go far, in school or who choose to pursue trades or less conventional careers. Some of these have little ability, others have considerable talent, though often in an area accorded comparatively little attention or prestige in most schools. In one way or another these young people are made to feel that they won't amount to anything: 'Let's face it, I'm no good. I'd like to do better, but I just don't get the stuff. I don't see any future for me. Everybody says you can't get anywhere without a college education these days. I just won't amount to anything.' Equally disturbing is: 'I know what I want is music—at least I used to be sure. I don't care how hard I work at it. But everybody tells me I'm foolish—that I'll starve—and why don't I wake up and go into my father's business. I wish they'd lay off.'

Madison Avenue's technique of repetition has been adopted—often for irreproachable reasons—to goad young people. Unfortunately, it convinced many not only that a college education is the *sine qua non* of a successful life but that material success is the goal and that without it they are destined to be useless, unhappy failures—that nothing else really counts. Caught up in this belief, schools emphasize the tools to success; and though not disparaging the cultivation of the virtues, or the arts, or the classics, they rarely allow these to interfere with what has increasingly become the major job.

Do, indeed, our preoccupations with material success and prestige, our pressures to excel, our reiteration that there is no future for those who do not do well academically, our emphasis on gaining the power knowledge yields and our neglect of the obligations it entails—do these combine to increase young people's emotional and behavioral problems, humiliate those who have little academic talent, and deny the cultivation of the virtues and the conscience their rightful priority? The inevitable anxiety which may be expected when standards are raised and demands on pupils are increased is a poor reason for advising a school day that offers little challenge: many pupils will find such anxiety no more than they can manage. So, too, can many handle the uncertainty created by their own questioning and searching, or by attempts to work out their own values and breathe new life into their heritage. However, when adolescents who have less ability but possess other admirable qualities are given but little support or hope, and seldom experience recognition or praise, then incapacitating worry, resentment, or passivity may be expected. It is one matter to urge that we all make our best effort, that we strive to reach our potential, and that we all seek knowledge, it is quite another to focus on success alone. If we are really concerned with these young people's futures it is essential to give as much recognition to those who have virtue as to those who have acquired knowledge, and to give more attention to what schools and teachers stand for, not just to the subjects they teach. At this impressionable, idealistic time of life, young people cannot have too many worthy examples to emulate. It would indeed be tragic if in our preoccupation to instill calculus we cultivated only calculating minds.

What *is* it that young people really need? What is it that these school years—both in and out of school—ought to yield them?

Primarily they need to feel that they belong in this world, that they have a place, that they are somebody. They need to experience the feeling that they are useful and competent in some area; they need to feel that others respect them. They need gradually to conquer their hostilities and to increase their capacity to care for others than themselves. The need for 'someone to love, a job to do, and something to look forward to' is as great today as it ever was. Otherwise, feelings of inferiority, resentment, a failure to realize potential, asocial behavior—all these and more are likely, if not inevitable.

Young people also need opportunities to work out their who-ness and their what-ness, their beliefs, their goals, their image of how they differ from everyone else. They need those who have traditionally had positions of respect to have the courage to take firm stands on what is right and what is wrong and to set a good example. They need opportunities to learn to live with and respect others, to learn to win and to lose, to have compassion, to have tolerance and yet to be themselves, to express and to control their feelings. They need someone whom they respect to listen to them. All this they need at a time of life when they are not only going through an adolescent's normal and desirable, though at times annoying, stages of physiologic and psychologic growth, but waxing and waning in the process. Their aims and attitudes vacillate too. Browning expressed their fluctuation between altruism and contempt succinctly in his 'I seemed to long at once to trample on, yet save mankind . . .'

They must, too, acquire a set of values, a mature conscience, and attitudes and beliefs about freedom, the law, and human dignity. They need to learn to care about people. They need to strengthen such old-fashioned virtues as mercy and honesty, generosity and compassion.

Young people find these things in the non-academic courses as well as in the academic ones, in their activities and at times frenzied strivings. The right people, the right experiences, the right books rub off on them: the *good* teacher teaches not only his subject but also himself—what *he* stands for.

The academically gifted also need, just as do the less able, more than their technical knowledge. A professor once explained why none of his excellent students would become a *great* astronomer: 'They don't love the stars.'

So it might be well for those who seek to modify the causes of the unhappy symptoms we see about us to try to counteract arrogance and those forces preoccupied with material success and power. And to try to prevent the development of those feelings of despair and worthlessness that may be instilled in those who do poorly in school. And to attempt to avoid increasing confusion in those adolescents torn between what they have been told was right and what they see done, and to save from bitter resentment or stultifying passivity those whose individuality is threatened with suppression. We all should strive for a wider appreciation of young people's need for encouragement and praise, of their susceptibility to people who respect them, and of their need for opportunities to be heard. We should work toward less focus on what adults often seem themselves to need adolescents to achieve. Out of our efforts might come a greater concern for adolescents' individuality, creativity, and compassion.

Finally, we should increasingly try to develop young people's awareness of their responsibilities, to instill the virtues and to elevate those who possess them, and to create more hope and respect and more places in our society for those good people without academic talent whom we now so often degrade.

For Further Reading

Arlitt, A. H., *The Adolescent* (New York: McGraw-Hill), 1938.

Bandura, A., and R. H. Walters, *Adolescent Aggression* (New York: Ronald Press), 1959.

Blaine, G. B., Jr., *The Parents' Guide to Adolescence* (Boston: Little, Brown), 1963.

Chapman, A. H., *Management of Emotional Problems of Children and Adolescents* (Philadelphia: Lippincott), 1965.

Doniger, Simon, *Becoming the Complete Adult* (New York: Association Press), 1962.

Dunbar, Flanders, *Your Teenager's Mind and Body* (New York: Hawthorne Books), 1962.

Edelston, H., *Problems of Adolescents* (London: Pitman Medical Publishing Co.), 1956.

Erikson, E. H., *Identity, Youth and Crisis* (New York: W. W. Norton), 1968.

Farnsworth, D., *Psychiatry, Education, and the Young Adult* (Springfield, Ill.: Charles C Thomas), 1966.

Farnham, M. F., *The Adolescent* (Mew York: Crowell-Collier), 1962.

Freud, A., Adolescence as a developmental disturbance, In G. Caplan and S. Lebovici (eds.), *Adolescence: Psychological Perspectives* (New York: Basic Books), 1969.

Gallagher, J. R., F. P. Heald, and D. C. Garell, *Medical Care of the Adolescent*, 3rd edition (New York: Appleton-Century-Crofts), 1975.

Garland, Joseph, *The Road to Adolescence* (Cambridge: Harvard University Press), 1934.

Glueck, S., and E. E. Glueck, *Toward a Typology of Juvenile Offenders* (New York: Grune & Stratton), 1970.

Gottlieb, Bernhardt S., *Understanding Your Adolescent* (New York: Rinehart), 1957.

Group for Advancement of Psychiatry, *Normal Adolescence: Its Dynamics and Impact* (New York: Scribners), 1968.

Guttmacher, A. F., *Understanding Sex: A Young Person's Guide* (New York: Harper & Row), 1970.

Hand, Learned, *The Spirit of Liberty* (New York: Knopf), 1952.

Hemming, J., *Problems of Adolescent Girls* (London: Heineman), 1960.

Hofmann, F. G. A *Handbook on Drug and Alcohol Abuse* (New York: Oxford University Press), 1975.

Holmes, D. J., *The Adolescent in Psychotherapy* (Boston: Little, Brown), 1964.

Jenkins, R. L., *Behavior Disorders of Adolescence* (Springfield, Ill.: Charles C Thomas), 1963.

Jersild, A. T., *The Psychology of Adolescence* (New York: Macmillan), 1957.

Josselyn, I. M., *Adolescence*, a report published under the auspices of the Joint Commission on Mental Health of Children (New York: Harper & Row), 1971.

Kiell, N., *The Universal Experience of Adolescence* (New York: International Universities Press), 1964.

Landis, Paul H., *Understanding Teen-Agers* (New York: Appleton-Century-Crofts), 1955.

Lorand, S., and H. I. Schneer, *Adolescents* (New York: Hoeber), 1961.

Masterson, J. F., *The Psychiatric Dilemma of Adolescence* (Boston: Little, Brown), 1967.

Meeks, J. E., *The Fragile Alliance: An Orientation to the Out-patient Psychotherapy of the Adolescent* (Baltimore: Williams & Wilkins), 1971.

Milner, Marion, *On Not Being Able to Paint* (London: Heinemann), 1971.

Odluim, D., *Journey Through Adolescence* (London: Penguin Books), 1957.

Pearson, Gerald H. J., *Adolescence and the Conflict of Generations* (New York: W. W. Norton), 1958.

————. *Psychoanalysis and the Education of the Child* (New York: W. W. Norton), 1954.

Schilder, P., *The Image and Appearance of the Human Body* (New York: International Universities Press), 1950.

Schoolar, J. C. (ed.), *Current Issues in Adolescent Psychiatry* (New York: Brunner/Mazell), 1973.

Spock, B., *Raising Children in a Difficult Time* (New York: Norton), 1974.

Symonds, P. M., *From Adolescent to Adult* (New York: Columbia University Press), 1961.

Thompson, L., *Reading Disability: Developmental Dyslexia* (Springfield, Ill.: Charles C Thomas), 1966.

U. S. Department of Health, Education and Welfare, The National Institute on Drug Abuse, *Marihuana and Health* (Washington, D.C., U. S. Government Printing Office), 1974.

———. U. S. Public Health Service, *Alcohol and Health* (Washington, D.C., U. S. Government Printing Office), 1974.

Waldborn, A. and H. Waldborn, *The Rite of Becoming* (New York: World Publishing Co.), 1969.

Index